Rewiring Your Brain

Cognitive Behavioral Therapy
Techniques for Anxiety Relief

Michelle Mann

Copyright © [Year of First Publication] by [Author or Pen Name]

All rights reserved.

No portion of this book may be reproduced in any form without written permission from the publisher or author, except as permitted by U.S. copyright law.

Contents

1. Introduction — 1
2. Understanding Anxiety — 15
3. The Principles of Cognitive Behavioral Therapy — 36
4. Mapping Your Anxiety — 53
5. Cognitive Techniques for Anxiety Management — 74
6. Behavioral Techniques for Anxiety Relief — 96
7. Advanced CBT Strategies — 105
8. Overcoming Obstacles in CBT — 117
9. CBT in Daily Life — 124
10. Technology and CBT — 139
11. Building a Support System — 147
12. Conclusion — 154
13. Gratitude Journal — 158

14.	Stress Management Plan	160
15.	How to Find a Qualified CBT Professional	162
16.	Recommended Reading	165

Introduction

In the fascinating world of neuroscience, the idea of neuroplasticity becomes a source of optimism, shedding light on how our brains work and their incredible ability to adapt during mental health challenges. Neuroplasticity highlights the brain's remarkable talent for rearranging itself, forming new pathways, and adjusting to different situations. This concept isn't just a scientific curiosity; it's making a meaningful impact on mental health, especially through the transformative lens of Cognitive Behavioral Therapy (CBT). CBT, tapping into the potential of neuroplasticity, emerges as a powerful ally in easing anxiety and addressing various psychological struggles.

Think of neuroplasticity as the brain's way of showing off its flexibility and adaptability. It's like a superhero power that lets the brain reshape itself, influenced by experiences, learning, and even therapeutic tricks. In the mental health realm, this adaptability becomes the key to unlocking some pretty impressive changes, especially when we team it up with intentional therapies like CBT. So, it's not just brain science jargon—it's the brain's own way of telling us it can transform for the better with a little help.

Cognitive Behavioral Therapy, commonly referred to as CBT, is a form of therapy that hinges on the principles of neuroplasticity. It is primarily based on the belief that our thoughts, feelings, and actions are the best of friends, always hanging out together and influencing one another. CBT seeks to tweak our not-so-great thought patterns, helping it to replace them with healthier mental habits. Think of it as a dance- CBT is brought in to shake things up, which creates new neural pathways. These pathways become the brain's cool new moves, helping you groove to life's stressors and challenges in a much more upbeat, positive way.

In this chapter, we will explore the scientific foundations of neuroplasticity, revealing how the inherent plasticity of the brain is a powerful ally in the journey to alleviate anxiety through CBT. As we explore this intricate dance between neural rewiring and therapeutic interventions, we will begin to understand the collaboration that exists between the transformative principles of CBT and the malleable nature of the brain.

In addition to exploring the scientific basis for CBT and neuroplasticity, we will also be sharing personal stories of individuals who have navigated the labyrinth of anxiety and emerged triumphant through the application of CBT. These stories are proof of the significant impact that the relationship between CBT and neuroplasticity can have on reshaping one's mental landscape.

Alright, buckle up! We're diving into the world of neuroplasticity and CBT together, ready to unravel the secrets behind how our brains adapt and the incredible magic that happens when we use it on purpose with CBT. But we're not just sticking to the science textbooks – we're throwing in some real-life stories, like treasures along the way. Our goal? To shine a light on the amazing changes that can happen when we blend brain science with the power of CBT. Consider this journey your personal guide, full of insights and inspiration for anyone cruising their own route to kick anxiety to the curb. Ready to roll? Let's go!

Understanding Neuroplasticity

Alright, let's break it down in everyday talk! Neuroplasticity is like the brain's superpower – this incredible ability to keep reshaping itself. Picture it as the brain making new connections between its neurons, kind of like rearranging furniture to fit the vibe of a room. And get this – it's not stuck in one way forever! Back in the day, people thought the brain's structure was set in stone after a certain age, but neuroplasticity busted that myth wide open. Now we know the brain is this adaptable champ, always ready for a makeover and a chance to change things up. Talk about a game-changer!

Many years ago, it was believed that the brain was rigid and static. Once someone was an adult, their brain connections were already in place and could not be changed. As research continued, it was discovered that this wasn't the case at all, and the concept of neuroplasticity emerged. Neuroplasticity showcases the dynamic nature of the brain, opening the door to innovative possibilities in mental health treatment. It challenges the restrictions of a predetermined structure, proving that the brain possesses an inherent capacity to grow and adapt throughout a person's life. This shift has a significant impact, especially in the realm of mental health, where the adaptability of the brain becomes a cornerstone for therapeutic interventions.

Think of your brain as the ultimate shapeshifter. It's this super adaptable maestro that's constantly fine-tuning itself in response to what you go through, what you learn, and the world around you. Neuroplasticity isn't just happening on one level; it's like a full-on symphony. From the tiniest tweaks in individual neurons to these grand rearrangements in the brain's complex networks, it's a dynamic process. This adaptability isn't just sitting pretty; it's a force that's got your back, helping you pick up new skills, bounce back from life's curveballs, and gracefully navigate the wild ride that is life.

Let's take a closer look: Imagine your brain's microscopic world, where individual neurons are like little architects, tweaking and adjusting in response to the vibes around them. This intricate dance, known as synaptic plasticity, is all about these neurons either tightening their bonds or taking a step back – a vital process for soaking in new knowledge and holding onto memories.

Now, if we zoom out a bit, it's like a grand reimagining happening on a larger scale. The brain's networks are creating new connections and saying goodbye to the ones that might need a break. It's the brain's way of staying nimble and ready for whatever adventures and challenges life throws its way. Think of it as a constant makeover to keep things fresh and adaptable.

Neuroplasticity isn't just a buzzword for brain scientists; it's making waves in the everyday world, especially in fields like psychology and mental health. Take Cognitive Behavioral Therapy (CBT), for example. It's like a perfect match with neuroplasticity – they're on the same team. CBT is all about helping you rethink those negative thoughts, and in doing so, it's like giving your brain a little makeover. It's like saying, "Hey brain, let's build some healthier paths up there!"

Understanding neuroplasticity changes how we see the brain. It's not this rigid thing; it's more like a superhero—resilient and able to make some serious changes. Imagine the brain as this ever-evolving wizard, not a boring old book with fixed pages. This way of thinking paints a picture where your brain isn't stuck; it's always got the potential for good stuff to happen, no matter how many birthdays you've had. Knowing this opens up exciting possibilities for mental health – it's like saying, "Hey brain, you're awesome, let's work together for some healing, growth, and bouncing back stronger than ever!"

How CBT Harnesses Neuroplasticity to Alleviate Anxiety

Cognitive Behavioral Therapy, or CBT, is a well-known therapeutic approach rooted in the belief that our thoughts, feelings, and behaviors are intertwined. The purpose of CBT is to identify and modify negative thought patterns and behaviors, providing individuals with practical tools to manage and overcome their anxiety.

Think of CBT and neuroplasticity as the ultimate power duo for your brain. It's not just therapy; it's like a dynamic dance where, as you practice CBT exercises and techniques, you're telling your brain, "Hey, let's switch things up!" You're actively encouraging your brain to build these stronger, healthier connections. It's not just about breaking the cycle of anxious thoughts and behaviors; it's like handing yourself a toolkit of savvy moves for dealing with whatever life throws your way. So, in this brain party, you're not just a guest – you're the star, calling the shots for a more adaptable and resilient mind.

CBT involves a variety of therapeutic techniques such as:

- Cognitive restructuring

- Behavioral exposure

- Mindfulness exercises

Research has shown that consistently practicing these interventions promotes changes in the neural pathways associated with anxiety. For example, challenging irrational thoughts and replacing them with more realistic ones leads to a restructuring of the cognitive processes of the brain, weakening the grip of anxiety-inducing patterns.

Of course, it is important to note that the transformative impact of CBT is not limited to the cognitive domain- it also extends into the emotional and behavioral areas as well. By addressing the root of your anxiety and providing you with practical coping mechanisms, CBT encourages the rewiring of the brain towards more positive, adaptive responses to stressors.

Personal Anecdotes of Triumph

While it is important to understand the science behind CBT, real-life stories are also important. They are proof that CBT is effective for reshaping the brain and overcoming anxiety.

Sarah

Allow me to introduce Sarah, a dynamic 32-year-old marketing professional whose journey with Cognitive Behavioral Therapy (CBT) has been nothing short of transformative. Sarah, a seasoned marketing whiz, discovered that CBT served as her mental boot camp, equipping her with the tools to identify and combat the negative thoughts that were perpetuating her anxiety.

In Sarah's words, CBT became a powerful process akin to reprogramming her brain. It wasn't just about acknowledging the existence of those intrusive and detrimental thoughts; it was about learning how to confront them head-on and reshape the cognitive landscape. Through dedicated practice and the guidance of CBT techniques, she gradually witnessed a profound shift in her thinking patterns.

Over time, the once-dominant force of anxiety began to lose its grip on Sarah's life. The constant barrage of negative thoughts that had previously dictated her emotions and actions was now being challenged and replaced with more rational and positive perspectives. Sarah's experience with CBT became a testament to the malleability of the human mind and its capacity for change.

For her, CBT wasn't merely a therapeutic approach; it was a holistic mental workout that strengthened her resilience and empowered her to reclaim control over her thoughts and emotions. The newfound clarity in her thinking ushered in a sense of liberation, as anxiety no longer called the shots in her daily life.

Sarah's journey with CBT serves as an inspiring narrative of personal growth and empowerment. It highlights the profound impact that targeted therapeutic interventions can have on reshaping one's mental landscape, allowing individuals to break free from the shackles of anxiety and forge a path towards a more positive and fulfilling life. In embracing the principles of CBT, Sarah not only transformed her relationship with negative thoughts but also discovered the resilience within herself to navigate life's challenges with newfound confidence and clarity.

John

Introducing John, a seasoned 40-year-old teacher who discovered a transformative ally in Cognitive Behavioral Therapy (CBT). In John's narrative, CBT emerged as his secret weapon, a dynamic tool wielded against the persistent challenges of stress and anxiety. His experience with CBT wasn't a tale of instant fixes or a magical cure; instead, it unfolded as a journey of practical exercises and mental reprogramming facilitated by his insightful therapist.

John found himself engaged in down-to-earth exercises that gradually rewired his brain's response to stress. These exercises were grounded in reality, reflecting the pragmatic essence of CBT. It wasn't about waving a magic wand to banish troubles; rather, it involved a step-by-step process, where the cumulative effect led to profound changes in how he approached and managed anxiety.

The transformative power of CBT, as John describes it, lies in the incremental victories. It's about taking the reins back from anxious thoughts, reclaiming control over one's mental landscape, and gradually shaping a new narrative. The journey with CBT, for John, became a process of self-discovery and empowerment, where he acquired practical tools to navigate the complexities of his own mind.

Bit by bit, John witnessed the subtle but powerful shifts in his mental well-being. The once-overwhelming grip of anxiety began to loosen, and life, in turn, felt like his own again. The exercises and strategies prescribed by his therapist in the realm of CBT became the building blocks for a renewed sense of agency and resilience.

John's experience with CBT serves as a testament to the real-world effectiveness of this therapeutic approach. It's not a quick fix, but a systematic and empowering process that equips individuals with the skills to confront and manage their thoughts and emotions. In embracing the principles of CBT, John not only regained control over his anxious thoughts but also rediscovered the joy of living life on his terms.

These personal stories prove that CBT isn't one-size-fits-all—it's like a custom-made suit, adapting to each person's quirks and struggles. Rewiring the brain? It's a slow dance, it requires both time and dedication. But what's so cool about these stories is that they're like little love letters to resilience. It's about folks finding this unexpected strength in themselves as they take on the journey to mental well-being.

Conclusion

Imagine neuroplasticity and Cognitive Behavioral Therapy (CBT) as your personal allies, shining a beacon of hope for anyone wading through the stormy waters of anxiety. In the vast, uncharted landscape of the brain's adaptability, CBT emerges like a trusted lighthouse, proving that therapy isn't just some distant concept—it's a real force that brings positive change. Dive into the stories of people like Sarah and John, and it's like witnessing a living miracle. Their tales echo the incredible potential of reshaping the mind, almost like a superhero shedding an old cape.

Think of the mental health journey as an epic adventure, with your brain playing the role of a superhero cape fluttering in the wind. The amazing knack your brain has for reshaping itself becomes a kind of secret weapon for anyone dealing with the twists and turns of anxiety. And the cool part? As science keeps uncovering new insights and therapy methods get even better, it's like the dynamic duo of neuroplasticity and CBT stepping into the spotlight, offering a hopeful path for anyone out there just hoping for a bit of relief from the anxiety rollercoaster.

Now, let's talk about Sarah. Her story is like watching a construction project on her mind—she's not just figuring things out; she's elbow-deep in a remodeling project. It's this unstoppable teamwork between neuroplasticity and CBT, pushing her toward a future that's not just brighter but more resilient than ever.

When there's John. His story is living proof that the mind can totally flex and bend with a little help from CBT. By picking up these better thinking habits and finding clever ways to deal with stuff, John rises above the drama of anxiety. Sarah and John's stories basically scream out that our minds, when teaming up with the tag duo of neuroplasticity and CBT, are like superheroes with this insane ability to heal and grow. It's pretty mind-blowing stuff.

As we dig into the complexities of anxiety and mental health, the connection between neuroplasticity and CBT looks like a promising beacon. It's an invitation not just to passively understand how our minds work but to actively join in the process of reshaping them. This intersection becomes a realm of possibility, where the ever-changing nature of the brain becomes a canvas for resilience, strength, and breaking free from the chains of anxiety. It's like discovering the superpowers within ourselves, not just to cope but to thrive and grow.

Understanding Anxiety

Anxiety is a universal companion in the human journey. It's like the uninvited guest crashing the party of our mental and emotional harmony. Picture it not just as a passing mood but as this persistent shadow, sneaking into every corner of your day, disrupting the delicate dance of daily life. When anxiety decides to set up camp for the long haul, it's no longer just a fleeting feeling; it becomes a constant companion, leaving its mark on every facet of your existence.

In its moderate form, anxiety is like that friend nudging you to stay sharp, a motivational force that kicks in when life throws challenges your way. But when it decides to overstay its welcome, anxiety transforms into something more potent, affecting not just your thoughts and feelings but your very way of being.

Rooted in the soil of excessive worry, fear, and the anticipation of what's to come, anxiety doesn't just stop at the mental realm. It spills over into the physical, leaving traces in the form of an accelerated heart rate, tense muscles, and an overall sense of restlessness. It's as if your body and mind are caught in this intricate dance with an unwelcome partner.

So, there it is – anxiety, not just a passing emotion, but a constant presence that shapes the narrative of your daily existence. It's the feeling of imbalance, the disrupted rhythm, and the shadow that clings to every step. Yet, in acknowledging its persistence, we begin the journey towards understanding, managing, and eventually finding ways to invite a bit more calmness and serenity back into our lives.

The Nature of Anxiety and its Effects on Life

Anxiety has a variety of effects on your life, including:

Physical Manifestations

Chronic anxiety is not just a headspace thing; it's a full-body takeover. Imagine this: your heart is doing a sprint, as if it's training for a marathon it never signed up for. Your muscles? Oh, they're flexed and tensed up, like they've been pumping iron in a never-ending gym session. And to top it off, this perpetual fidgetiness that just won't quit – it's like being stuck in a restless dance you never asked to be a part of.

Now, these aren't just your body's way of reacting to perceived threats; they're more like those unwelcome guests that show up uninvited and decide to stick around for an extended stay. It's like your body and mind are hosting a party you never planned, and these symptoms, well, they add an extra layer of unease and discomfort to the whole experience.

So, chronic anxiety isn't just this abstract concept; it's a tangible, physical presence that infiltrates every inch of your being. It's the heartbeats in overdrive, the muscles stuck in a perpetual flex, and the feeling that you're in a never-ending jittery dance. Acknowledging these physical manifestations is a crucial step in understanding the depth of the experience and, ultimately, finding ways to ease the grip of these unwelcome guests on your day-to-day life.

Disruptions in Sleep Patterns

Living with chronic anxiety takes a toll on more than just your feelings; it really messes with your sleep too. Imagine this: a mind that just won't hush, thoughts racing like they're in a marathon of their own. It's like trying to catch some **shut eye** with a mental circus playing in the background. Falling asleep becomes this elusive goal, and even when you do manage it, staying asleep feels like balancing on a tightrope.

Now, the sleep disruptions don't just stop at being annoying; they play into this whole anxiety loop. Lack of quality sleep piles up fatigue, making it even trickier to handle the stressors life throws your way. It's this cruel cycle where anxiety messes with your sleep, and the resulting fatigue makes it even harder to manage the very stressors that fuel the anxiety in the first place.

So, chronic anxiety isn't just about being in a constant mental race; it's like trying to catch some quality z's in the middle of a noisy carnival. The struggle to find peaceful sleep becomes a part of the larger battle against anxiety, each playing into the other and making it all the more challenging to break free from the grip of this relentless cycle.

Concentration Difficulties

Dealing with anxiety isn't just a mental hurdle; it can seriously mess with your ability to concentrate. Imagine this: a persistent background noise of worry and nervousness that makes focusing feel like trying to tune into a single radio station in the middle of a crowded frequency. People grappling with anxiety might find it tough to direct their attention, make decisions, or tackle tasks that need some serious concentration.

It's like your mind is hosting its own racing thoughts marathon, making it a real challenge to stay in the moment and give your full attention to whatever you're working on. This cognitive fog isn't just a minor inconvenience; it's a genuine roadblock that slows down productivity and can lead to some serious frustration. Imagine trying to juggle all your mental tasks while feeling like your cognitive capacity is playing hide and seek – it's not exactly a walk in the park.

So, anxiety, in addition to being this constant undercurrent of worry, is also like a mischievous imp messing with your ability to focus. It's not just about feeling a bit distracted; it's about wrestling with a mental wrestling match that can leave you feeling drained and a bit defeated. Understanding this impact on concentration is a crucial step in navigating the complexities of anxiety and finding ways to regain control over your cognitive prowess.

Fatigue and Overall Well-being

Anxiety isn't just a mind game; it's a whole-body experience that can knock the wind out of your well-being sails. Imagine this: your stress button getting a workout that never seems to end. It's like running a marathon, except you never even laced up your sneakers. The impact doesn't stop at a simple feeling of tiredness; it's more like this constant drain on your energy, leaving you feeling like you've been through the wringer.

Picture your body as this intricate machine, and anxiety as the persistent force turning the cogs at full speed. Your shoulders might carry the weight of the world, your stomach might feel like it's doing somersaults, and even the simplest tasks can feel like scaling a mountain. It's not just a mental weariness; it's a bone-deep, soul-tugging exhaustion that becomes a daily companion.

So, when we talk about anxiety impacting overall well-being, it's not just about feeling a bit off—it's about feeling like you've been through the wringer, body and soul. Recognizing this toll on your physical and mental energy is a crucial step in acknowledging the complexities of anxiety and working towards restoring a sense of balance and vitality in your life.

Impact on Relationships

Let's talk about anxiety as more than just a solo mission—it's like a party-crasher that has a knack for affecting your connections with others. Picture this: the relentless worry battle that you're fighting becomes a tag-along in your interactions with friends, family, and colleagues. It's not just about you, it's like anxiety sneaks into the room, casting a shadow on the dynamics that were once carefree.

People wrestling with anxiety might find it tricky to be fully present in social situations. It's not for lack of wanting; it's like there's this invisible barrier that makes engaging in conversations and connecting with others feel like trying to dance in shoes two sizes too big. The struggle to show up authentically in social interactions leads to a sense of isolation, creating this echo chamber where anxiety thrives, and your mental well-being takes another hit.

So, when we say anxiety impacts interpersonal relationships, it's not just a theoretical idea—it's a real, lived experience. It's those missed connections, the unspoken tension, and the feeling of being on the outskirts of your own social world. Acknowledging this ripple effect on relationships is crucial in understanding the multi-faceted nature of anxiety and finding ways to nurture connections despite the challenging dance it introduces into our social lives.

Occupational Challenges

Workplace anxiety is not just a mental hurdle; it's like having an uninvited companion at your career table. Picture this: you're in the thick of your professional journey, juggling deadlines, and striving for career milestones, but there it is—a constant companion named worry, pulling up a chair and refusing to budge. It's not just a fleeting concern; it's like having this persistent tag-along that shadows your every move.

Concentration becomes this delicate tightrope walk, where you're trying to balance the demands of your job with the incessant hum of anxious thoughts in the background. It's like performing a high-wire act with your focus, where one misstep could lead to a cascade of worries. And let's talk about productivity—it takes a hit. It's not for lack of effort; it's the challenge of trying to deliver your best work when your mental space is crowded with worry.

So, in the workplace, anxiety isn't just a concept; it's a real, daily struggle that accompanies you to meetings, deadlines, and coffee breaks. It's the unexpected guest at the career table, influencing your decisions, your interactions, and your ability to climb the professional ladder. Recognizing this impact is a crucial step in navigating the complexities of workplace anxiety and finding strategies to carve out a space where both your career and mental well-being can thrive.

Understanding anxiety is akin to discovering a roadmap that helps you navigate life's unpredictable twists and turns. It's not just about grasping the ups and downs of an emotional rollercoaster; it's about recognizing the comprehensive spectrum of effects it casts upon your day-to-day existence. Consider it your personal toolkit – the more insights you uncover, the better prepared you become to navigate the labyrinth of emotions.

Managing anxiety isn't a plunge into the deep end of emotions; it's a process that involves addressing the tangible, practical, and physical consequences that tag along. Picture it like gently unraveling a stubborn knot – you meticulously work on each strand to find relief in various aspects of your life. So, understanding anxiety is more than just putting a name to the emotion; it's about acknowledging its far-reaching impact on your entire world. It's about seeking the right support and adopting strategies that resonate with you, enabling you to skillfully navigate through life's challenges.

Diverse Types of Anxiety Disorders

Anxiety disorders aren't cut from the same cloth; they're more like a vibrant kaleidoscope, each presenting a unique tapestry of persistent and overwhelming worry. It's not just a simple case of feeling stressed – it's about embracing the diverse spectrum of these disorders, each with its own intricate set of challenges.

Picture it as navigating through a rich and varied landscape; to truly comprehend it, you've got to delve into the distinct features and expressions of each anxiety disorder. It's like peeling back layers of an intricate artwork, revealing the subtle nuances that shape the experience. This way, you can tailor your approach to managing your mental health with a clearer understanding of the specific challenges that come with each disorder. It's about recognizing the individuality within the realm of anxiety and finding a more human-centric approach to navigate the intricacies of mental well-being.

Generalized Anxiety Disorder (GAD)

Generalized Anxiety Disorder, **or** GAD **is like** having a mental playlist, but instead of catchy tunes, it's filled with worry tracks that just won't quit. With GAD, it's like your mind cranks up the volume on anxiety, and suddenly, everyday concerns become these looming shadows that overshadow everything else.

It's not your run-of-the-mill worries about work, family, or health; it's like your brain decided to host an anxiety Olympics, where even the smallest of concerns get gold medals. Picture this: you're trying to enjoy a simple cup of coffee, but your mind is busy crafting scenarios of what could go wrong at work tomorrow or what might happen in the distant future.

This persistent and excessive worrying isn't just a fleeting concern—it's a constant companion. It's the mental equivalent of having a buzzing background noise that follows you everywhere, making it tough to catch a break. Everyday tasks that used to be a breeze suddenly feel like trying to navigate a maze blindfolded.

Living with GAD means your mind is in a perpetual whirlwind of 'what if' scenarios. It's not about being stressed occasionally; it's about feeling on edge about a bunch of things almost all the time. If it seems like your mind is stuck in a loop of worrying about the future, no matter how hard you try to hit pause, that might be the signature of Generalized Anxiety Disorder. Understanding it is the first step toward finding ways to turn down the worry volume and regain a sense of peace in your daily life.

Panic Disorder

Imagine your body as a car, and suddenly, without any warning, the alarm goes off, and the engine revs up like crazy. Your heart pounds, you start sweating, and it feels like you're in an emergency, even though there's no real danger around.

That's what it's like for someone with Panic Disorder. These "panic attacks" come out of the blue and make you feel like you're in the middle of a wild rollercoaster ride. It's not just feeling nervous or scared – it's a sudden surge of intense physical sensations that can be overwhelming.

Sometimes, people might start avoiding certain places or situations because they worry it'll trigger another panic attack. It's like trying to steer clear of that unpredictable car alarm. But here's the thing: even though panic attacks are super intense, they're not dangerous. It's like a false alarm, but your body reacts as if it's a real emergency.

So, Panic Disorder is like having this unexpected car alarm in your body that goes off out of the blue, making you feel like you're in an emergency, even when everything is okay. Understanding it helps folks navigate through the experience and find ways to manage these sudden, intense moments.

Social Anxiety Disorder

Imagine you're at a big party, and instead of feeling excited to chat with people, you feel super nervous and worried about what others might think of you. Social Anxiety Disorder is like having these extra-strong butterflies in your stomach when you're around others.

It's not just being shy or feeling a bit awkward; it's like your mind hits the panic button in social situations. You might worry a lot about saying something wrong, being judged, or embarrassing yourself. Even everyday activities like speaking in class, going to a party, or making a phone call can feel like stepping onto a stage with a spotlight on you.

People with social anxiety might avoid social situations altogether to escape that uncomfortable feeling. It's like trying to dodge the big party because you're worried it'll be too nerve-wracking. But here's the good news: with understanding and support, many folks find ways to manage these anxious feelings and feel more comfortable in social settings. Social Anxiety Disorder is just a part of who someone is, and there are ways to work through it and still enjoy social interactions.

Specific Phobias

Specific phobias are a bit like having your own collection of fear magnets – these intense and irrational fears that can range from heights to spiders, flying, or anything else that sends shivers down your spine. These aren't just your everyday worries; they unleash a full-blown fear response that turns even the simplest tasks into high-stakes challenges.

Picture it as navigating a world where these fear magnets are hiding around every corner, ready to pounce and set off a storm of anxiety. It's not just about feeling a bit uneasy; it's like being on a constant quest to avoid these anxiety triggers. The impact of specific phobias can vary, from dealing with manageable discomfort to facing a profound restriction in your daily activities.

Living with specific phobias is like having this invisible companion that influences how you move through the world. It's a delicate dance of steering clear of triggers, trying to maintain a balance between your fears and the desire to live a fulfilling life. Each day becomes a journey of facing and navigating these fear magnets, finding ways to cope, and gradually reclaiming the reins from the invisible force that seeks to dictate your movements.

Obsessive-Compulsive Disorder (OCD)

Imagine your brain is like a radio station, and sometimes, it gets stuck on a particular thought or tune. With OCD, these thoughts are called "obsessions," and they're like unwanted, repetitive radio tracks that won't change.

To deal with these thoughts, your brain comes up with certain actions or rituals, known as "compulsions." It's like trying to change the radio station by doing a specific routine or checking things repeatedly. For example, if you're worried about germs, you might feel the need to wash your hands over and over.

The tricky part is, even though you might know these thoughts or actions don't make much sense, it's tough to turn off the mental radio or resist the urge to perform these rituals. It's like a mental loop that plays over and over, and the compulsions become a way to cope with the anxiety caused by the obsessions.

Living with OCD can be challenging, but with understanding, support, and sometimes professional help, many people find effective ways to manage these unwanted thoughts and behaviors, turning down the volume on the mental radio and regaining a sense of control.

Post-Traumatic Stress Disorder (PTSD)

Imagine you've been through something really tough, like a scary event that felt life-threatening. Now, instead of moving on easily, your mind gets stuck on that moment, and it keeps replaying like a loop.

With PTSD, it's like your brain gets stuck on a particular channel, bringing back memories, nightmares, or even physical reactions when something reminds you of that difficult time. These can be things like loud sounds, certain smells, or even situations that trigger those memories.

It's not just remembering; it's like reliving the tough experience over and over, and it can make you feel really on edge, anxious, or even disconnected from the present. Everyday things might suddenly feel dangerous or overwhelming.

But the good news is, with support and understanding, many people find ways to cope with these tough memories and start to feel more in control of their thoughts and emotions. It's like slowly changing the channel from the difficult loop and finding a more peaceful space within your own mind.

Embracing the distinctive features of each anxiety disorder is like uncovering a personalized map that guides us towards accurate diagnosis and tailor-made treatment. It goes beyond mere labels; it's about delving into the unique hurdles that each individual encounters within the vast spectrum of anxiety disorders.

Imagine it as creating a bespoke key for every lock, acknowledging the shared thread of anxiety while attentively recognizing the nuanced details that make each condition stand out. This personalized approach isn't just a task for mental health professionals; it's a collaborative venture between them and individuals, forging a path for interventions that are not only effective but precisely honed to address specific challenges.

It's a journey towards healing and resilience, one that places immense value on the individuality of each person's experience with anxiety. In this shared exploration, the road to recovery becomes a finely tuned instrument, resonating with the unique needs, strengths, and complexities that shape the mental health landscape for each person.

The Brain Chemistry of Anxiety and its Triggers

Navigating the world of anxiety takes us into the intricate dance of the brain's circuitry, where neurotransmitters like serotonin, GABA, and norepinephrine play pivotal roles in shaping our mood and anxiety levels. It's like a symphony, with each neurotransmitter contributing to the delicate balance that governs how we experience and manage anxiety.

Imagine these neurotransmitters as the conductors of an orchestra, influencing the ebb and flow of emotions. When the harmony is disrupted, when there's an imbalance, that's where the intricate story of anxiety begins.

Understanding this dance, this interplay, helps us unravel the neurobiological tapestry that underlies anxiety disorders – a journey into the very essence of our brain's inner workings.

Picture the amygdala as the emotional maestro of your brain, orchestrating responses to the world around you. Nestled in the folds of your brain, this conductor, when it comes to anxiety, plays a crucial role. It's like the radar for threat detection, processing stimuli that set off the body's stress alarms.

For those grappling with anxiety, the amygdala might take center stage a bit too eagerly, showing signs of hyperactivity. It's as if the emotional maestro gets a little too carried away, amplifying emotional responses to everyday stimuli. Understanding this behind-the-scenes drama in the brain gives us a glimpse into the complex symphony of emotions that individuals with anxiety navigate daily.

Think of anxiety as a puzzle, and life experiences, genetics, and your environment are all pieces that come together to create the picture. Traumatic events or the persistent hum of chronic stress can add complexity to this puzzle, making some individuals more vulnerable to anxiety. It's like having a unique set of puzzle pieces based on your family history; if anxiety is a familiar presence, it might be part of your puzzle.

Your personality also plays a role in this intricate picture. Imagine traits like perfectionism or a penchant for seeing the glass half empty as colors on your palette. They add their hues to the canvas, influencing how anxiety takes shape. In this way, understanding anxiety becomes not just unravelling a puzzle but appreciating the artistry of individual experiences and traits that shape our mental landscape.

Think of triggers as the keys that unlock the door to anxiety. They're like a diverse cast of characters, ranging from external situations to the thoughts buzzing within your mind. Imagine your brain as a stage where these triggers perform, and knowing how they interact with your unique chemistry is like having a front-row seat.

By recognizing these triggers, it's akin to understanding the script of your anxiety. Some scenes may be set off by external events, while others are crafted from the inner dialogue you have with yourself. Picture this understanding as a powerful flashlight, illuminating the path to effective anxiety management. It's not just about turning the spotlight on the triggers; it's about crafting a narrative that allows you to navigate the story of your anxiety with insight and resilience.

In this chapter, we have explored the multi-faceted nature of anxiety, exploring its impact on your daily life, the spectrum of anxiety-based disorders, and the intricate workings of brain chemistry that underlie this complex phenomenon. By understanding the intricacies of anxiety, individuals and mental health professionals can navigate the path toward the creation and application of effective interventions and improved well-being.

The Principles of Cognitive Behavioral Therapy

Cognitive Behavioral Therapy (CBT) is a pioneer in the vast landscape of psychotherapy, an architect weaving together the threads of cognition and behavior into a vibrant tapestry of transformative mental health interventions. It's not just a therapeutic approach; it's a narrative that unfolds through history, with its roots tracing back to the mid-20th century.

Imagine walking alongside trailblazers like Albert Ellis and Aaron T. Beck, explorers of the human psyche who, with their pioneering spirits, illuminated new paths in understanding and treating mental health. CBT isn't just a set of techniques; it's a living story, enriched by the experiences and wisdom of those who ventured into the complexities of the mind, forging a way forward for generations seeking solace and growth.

In the 1950s, Albert Ellis pioneered a new path, crafting the initial pathways with the introduction of Rational Emotive Behavior Therapy, or REBT. Ellis, a trailblazer in the realm of psychotherapy, laid the groundwork for a transformative paradigm that would redefine how we understand and address emotional challenges.

At the heart of Ellis's groundbreaking approach was a profound realization—the immense power of irrational beliefs in shaping our emotional responses. Ellis invited individuals to embark on a journey of self-discovery, encouraging them to challenge and reframe these irrational beliefs. This departure from traditional psychoanalytic methods marked a shift towards empowerment, providing people with tangible tools to actively reshape their cognitive landscapes. Ellis's legacy is not just a historical footnote; it's a testament to the human capacity for growth and transformation, echoing through the decades and resonating with those seeking a more resilient and adaptive emotional journey.

Now, let's journey into the dynamic landscape of the 1960s, a time of revolutionary ideas and cultural shifts. In this era, the visionary Aaron T. Beck took the reins, steering the course of psychotherapy into uncharted territories with the emergence of Cognitive Therapy.

Beck's approach was a departure from conventional thinking, placing a spotlight on the intricate dance between thoughts and emotions. He shifted the narrative, suggesting that it was not the events themselves but our interpretations that held the key to emotional distress. In essence, he handed individuals the compass to navigate their cognitive landscapes.

Picture this as an expedition of self-discovery where individuals, guided by Beck's innovative techniques, unravelled and challenged their cognitive distortions. The goal was clear—by recalibrating their thoughts, they could alleviate emotional distress and forge a path to mental well-being. Beck's influence reverberates through time, an enduring legacy that echoes the empowerment of individuals in understanding and reshaping their emotional narratives.

Imagine a meeting of minds, a crossroads in the world of psychotherapy where two distinct approaches found common ground. Albert Ellis, with his emphasis on belief systems, and Aaron T. Beck, unravelling the intricacies of cognitive distortions, embarked on a collaborative journey. It was a fusion of ideas, a dance of perspectives, culminating in the birth of something transformative—Cognitive Behavioral Therapy (CBT).

This was no ordinary merger; it was a harmonious blend that addressed the complex tapestry of human psychology. Ellis's Rational Emotive Behavior Therapy seamlessly intertwined with Beck's Cognitive Therapy, creating a holistic modality that embraced both cognitive and behavioral dimensions of well-being. Picture it as the birth of a dynamic therapeutic force—one that would go on to shape the narratives of countless individuals, offering a path to understanding and healing that transcended the boundaries of traditional psychotherapy.

In the intricate tapestry of mental health, Cognitive Behavioral Therapy (CBT) emerges as a guiding light, weaving together cognitive and behavioral threads into a transformative fabric. The roots of CBT delve into the mid-20th century, where pioneers like Albert Ellis and Aaron T. Beck paved the way for a revolutionary approach. Ellis, in the 1950s, introduced Rational Emotive Behavior Therapy (REBT), highlighting the influence of irrational beliefs on emotions. Building upon this foundation, Beck's Cognitive Therapy in the 1960s focused on reshaping distorted thought patterns. These two paths eventually converged to give birth to the dynamic and comprehensive modality we now know as CBT.

In the captivating saga of psychotherapy's evolution, Cognitive Behavioral Therapy (CBT) emerges as a beacon of transformative potential. A fusion of rational-emotive principles and cognitive restructuring, CBT not only signifies a historical milestone but a vibrant legacy. It invites individuals into a journey of profound self-discovery, offering a transformative path to understand, challenge, and reshape their thoughts, emotions, and behaviors—ushering them toward enduring mental well-being.

Core Principles of CBT and How It Addresses Anxiety

In the realm of psychotherapy, Cognitive Behavioral Therapy (CBT) emerges as a compassionate guide, rooted in principles that acknowledge the intricate choreography of thoughts, emotions, and behaviors. Think of it as a comforting beacon that lights up the path toward understanding the complex dance within our minds and hearts.

At its essence, CBT gently whispers the wisdom that our perceptions and interpretations of situations hold the power to shape our emotional responses and actions. It's like acknowledging that the lens through which we view the world can color our experiences. Now, when it comes to tackling anxiety, CBT becomes this supportive ally, working on the fundamental belief that our thinking patterns, especially those that tend to be distorted or negative, act as triggers for the heightened levels of anxiety we experience.

In simpler terms, it's like CBT is helping us unravel the stories our minds tell us. These stories, often shaped by anxiety, might not always reflect reality. CBT steps in to reshape these narratives, offering a kind of mental renovation that allows for more balanced and realistic thinking. It's not just a therapy; it's a journey of understanding and rewiring, where thoughts are recognized, gently questioned, and nudged toward a healthier, more empowering perspective.

Cognitive Restructuring: Unveiling the Power of Thought Modification

Right at the core of CBT's way of dealing with anxiety, there's this thing called cognitive restructuring. Think of it as a mental makeover where we roll up our sleeves and get to work on those irrational thoughts that love to crank up the anxiety volume. It's like being a detective, spotting those tricky thoughts that aren't playing fair, and giving them a reality check.

Now, here comes the fun part – we're not just pointing fingers at those distorted thoughts; we're swapping them out. Imagine trading your anxiety-inducing thoughts for more down-to-earth and balanced perspectives. It's like putting on a new pair of glasses that see the world with a clearer, more realistic view. This intentional tweak to the way you think isn't just a mind game; it's like setting off a chain reaction.

Changing up those thought patterns sends ripples through the emotional pond. Suddenly, the way you feel about situations starts to shift. It's not a magical transformation, but it's like adjusting the dial on your emotional responses. And guess what happens next? This ripple effect extends to your actions, creating a whole new dance with anxiety. It's not just about thinking differently; it's about rewriting the script of how you respond to the anxiety tango.

Behavioral Techniques: Confronting Anxiety Head-On

Alright, let's dive into the nuts and bolts of CBT, where exposure therapy and behavioral activation take center stage in the battle against anxiety. These are like the heavy-hitters, the superheroes in the CBT playbook.

First up, we have exposure therapy – the real MVP. Imagine it as a carefully crafted strategy where you face up to situations that usually make your anxiety do somersaults. But here's the catch – it's not a full-speed-ahead plunge; it's more like dipping your toes into the anxiety pool in a slow and controlled manner. It's a strategic showdown with anxiety triggers that goes beyond just toughening up; it's about building resilience. It's like training your mind to dial down the impact of those anxiety-inducing moments, one controlled exposure at a time.

Now, let's chat about another game-changer in the CBT toolkit – behavioral activation. This one is like a compass pointing you toward positive vibes. Instead of getting entangled in the anxiety loop of dodging and withdrawing, behavioral activation encourages you to dive into activities that bring joy, satisfaction, and a sense of accomplishment.

It's like breaking free from anxiety's grip and creating a ripple effect of healthier responses and a brighter mindset.

So, in the CBT playbook, it's not just about facing fears and diving into activities – it's a dynamic strategy that equips you with the tools to reshape your relationship with anxiety, fostering resilience and steering your mindset toward a sunnier outlook.

Coping Skills: Empowering Individuals on their Anxiety Journey

Imagine CBT as your trusted companion, not just navigating through anxiety but ushering you into a realm of practical wisdom. It's not about waving a magic wand; it's about rolling up your sleeves and learning the ropes. In CBT, you're not relegated to the role of a mere passenger; instead, you become an active participant in acquiring and wielding coping skills.

These skills aren't just lifeless tools; they're like steadfast companions on your journey, offering a helping hand in managing stress, grappling with negative thoughts, and facing triggers with newfound resilience. They're not merely skills; they're your reliable sidekicks, making the winding path through anxiety a bit more manageable and less daunting.

Think of CBT not just as a set of techniques but as your personal guide on this holistic journey to tackle anxiety. It's like having a reliable friend by your side, assisting you in reshaping your thoughts, confronting fears head-on, and cultivating positive behaviors. CBT isn't just a toolkit; it's a compass, pointing you toward resilience, understanding, and enduring well-being. It's not solely about breaking free from anxiety; it's about forging a path to a more resilient and fulfilling life, where you're equipped with the tools and insights to navigate challenges with a newfound strength.

The Evidence Base for CBT's Effectiveness in Treating Anxiety

Let's dive into why CBT isn't just your run-of-the-mill treatment; it's a steadfast ally in the ongoing battle against anxiety, and it's got the evidence to back it up. Countless studies have taken CBT through its paces, and guess what? The results are in, and they're shouting it from the rooftops: CBT works, plain and simple.

Whether you're wrestling with generalized anxiety disorder, grappling with panic attacks, navigating the challenges of social anxiety, or facing down your unique set of phobias, CBT is like a versatile Swiss Army knife for your mental well-being. It's not a one-size-fits-all approach; it's tailor-made to adapt to your personal struggles, providing relief when you need it most.

It's not just therapy; it's a proven path, grounded in science, toward loosening the crippling grip of anxiety. Think of CBT as that reliable friend who's been through the trenches and emerged stronger. It's not just about managing symptoms; it's about reclaiming a sense of control and finding a way forward, armed with the insights and tools that make a real difference in your daily life.

Scientific Endorsement through Clinical Trials

Imagine CBT as a seasoned companion, battle-tested in the trenches of clinical trials, showcasing its prowess against a range of anxiety disorders. It's like that steadfast friend who knows the ins and outs, capable of easing the burden of excessive worry in generalized anxiety and slamming the brakes on panic attacks.

These trials aren't just dry studies; they're living proof of CBT's versatility and resilience when confronted with the challenges posed by anxiety. It's not merely a therapy; it's a tried-and-true method, a reliable guide that has demonstrated its ability to navigate the intricate landscape of anxiety.

Picture CBT as your seasoned guide, someone who has faced the complexities of anxiety head-on and emerged victorious. It's not just about managing symptoms; it's about journeying together towards a place of understanding, empowerment, and tangible relief from the grip of anxiety. In the realm of mental well-being, CBT stands not just as a theoretical concept but as a proven, compassionate companion offering real solutions to the challenges that anxiety presents.

Lasting Improvements and Comparable Efficacy

Research vividly illustrates how CBT isn't just a quick fix for anxiety—it's more like a lasting embrace of relief. It's akin to discovering a steadfast companion on your journey against anxiety, someone who doesn't just offer momentary respite but provides enduring benefits that often surpass the effects of medication alone.

In the landscape of mental well-being, CBT stands out not merely as a solution but as a reliable anchor. It goes beyond just addressing symptoms; it offers a sustained sense of ease and freedom from the clutches of anxiety. It's like having a trusted ally by your side, navigating the twists and turns of your mental health journey and providing ongoing support that transcends the transient nature of many interventions.

Imagine CBT as a reassuring presence, not just swooping in for a brief moment of relief but offering a continuous source of strength. It's not about masking the symptoms; it's about fundamentally transforming your relationship with anxiety, fostering a sense of resilience, and paving the way for a more liberated and fulfilled life.

Adaptability Across Anxiety Disorders

Imagine CBT as your personalized craftsman, not dishing out generic remedies but intricately sculpting solutions tailored just for you in the complex puzzle of anxiety. It's like having an artisan who doesn't believe in one-size-fits-all, but instead, delicately shapes each piece to fit your unique mental landscape.

The remarkable thing about CBT is its ability to adapt and flex, like a skilled dancer responding to the unique rhythm of each anxiety disorder. Whether it's untangling the knot of worrisome thoughts in Generalized Anxiety Disorder (GAD) or gently guiding you through the labyrinth of fears in various phobias, CBT isn't just about treating; it's about tailoring.

Picture it as a dance, a therapeutic waltz that twirls and sways with the intricacies of your individual anxiety journey. CBT doesn't impose; it partners with you, learning the steps of your unique dance and helping you navigate the twists and turns with grace and precision. It's not a rigid formula but a fluid collaboration, a customized approach that acknowledges and respects the distinct patterns of your anxiety puzzle.

Beyond Symptom Reduction: Quality of Life and Functionality

CBT is more than a checklist of symptoms; it's like opening a window to a brighter, more vibrant life. Those who embark on the CBT journey often discover that it's not just about managing anxiety but stepping into a world where daily activities transform into vibrant, meaningful experiences. It's like rediscovering the joy in the little things, savoring each moment as if seeing the world through a new lens.

Beyond the mechanics of fixing what feels broken, CBT becomes a trusted guide, leading the way to a life that's not just about surviving but thriving. It's not a rigid set of rules but a dynamic journey where individuals find the space to explore and embrace a richer, more fulfilling existence. With CBT, it's not just about coping with anxiety; it's about unlocking the door to a life that radiates with vitality, purpose, and the simple pleasures that make each day special.

Reduced Likelihood of Relapse: A Testament to Long-Term Efficacy

CBT is not just a fleeting remedy but a reliable anchor, a sturdy companion for the journey that lies ahead. What sets it apart is its ability to provide more than just immediate relief—it's akin to constructing a fortress against the potential return of anxiety. Those who welcome CBT into their lives discover that it equips them not just for the challenges of today but for the multitude of tomorrows, arming them with the tools to navigate life's twists and turns with newfound resilience.

It's not a quick fix, but a lasting transformation, like a beacon that continues to shine even after the therapy sessions conclude. CBT becomes a foundation, a steady presence that individuals can lean on as they navigate the ebbs and flows of life. It's not just about managing anxiety in the present; it's about crafting a lasting strategy, a robust set of skills that individuals carry with them, serving as a compass for their ongoing journey towards mental well-being.

Unveiling the Transformative Force of CBT

As we bring this chapter to a close, it's crucial to recognize that Cognitive Behavioral Therapy isn't a mere collection of abstract ideas on paper; it's a potent fusion of theory and practice, a toolbox brimming with strategies deeply rooted in tangible, real-world results. The solid foundation laid by clinical trials and extensive research isn't just professional jargon; it stands as a testament to CBT's authentic impact on mental health.

By delving into its origins, grasping its fundamental principles, and appreciating the robust evidence supporting its efficacy, we uncover CBT's pivotal role in addressing anxiety. It's not confined to the realm of symptom relief; rather, it serves as a guiding force, leading individuals on a transformative journey towards enduring well-being and resilience.

Think of CBT not as an abstract concept but as a trusted companion, offering practical tools that extend beyond the theoretical realm. It's not just about understanding the theory; it's about experiencing the tangible benefits in daily life. CBT becomes a dynamic force, not only helping individuals navigate the complexities of anxiety but also providing a roadmap toward a more robust, enduring mental well-being.

Mapping Your Anxiety

Understanding the details of your anxiety is critical for effective management and recovery. In this chapter, we will explore a variety of techniques to help you chart and understand your personal anxiety patterns. By recognizing your patterns, you gain valuable insights into the triggers, thought patterns, and behaviors that are involved in your anxiety. It's like creating a personalized map for your journey of managing and overcoming anxiety.

3 Tools For Mapping and Managing Anxiety

Below, we'll explore 3 tools you can use to map and manage your anxiety:

Journaling/Self-Reflection

Journaling or self-reflection can be a powerful tool in managing anxiety. Here are several ways in which this practice can be beneficial:

- Expression of Emotions: Writing allows individuals to express their thoughts and emotions in a safe and private space. It provides an outlet to unload the weight of anxious feelings, helping to release pent-up emotions.

- Increased Self-Awareness: Journaling encourages self-reflection, leading to a better understanding of the patterns and triggers associated with anxiety. By identifying these factors, individuals can work towards managing them more effectively.

- Identification of Triggers: Through regular journaling, individuals may notice recurring themes or situations that trigger their anxiety. This awareness can empower them to develop coping strategies or seek support when needed.

- Problem Solving: Writing about anxiety-inducing situations can help individuals explore potential solutions. It allows them to think more objectively and come up with practical ways to address challenges, fostering a sense of control.

- Tracking Progress: Journaling provides a tangible record of an individual's journey. By reviewing past entries, one can observe patterns of growth, recognize achievements, and acknowledge moments of resilience, offering a positive perspective on progress.

- Mindfulness and Present Moment Awareness: Writing can be a form of mindfulness, encouraging individuals to focus on the present moment. This practice can help ground them in reality, diverting attention away from anxious thoughts about the future.

- Release of Negative Thoughts: Journaling allows individuals to confront and release negative thoughts onto paper. This process can be cathartic, helping to prevent the buildup of destructive thought patterns.

- Goal Setting: Setting small, achievable goals and documenting progress in a journal can be empowering. It shifts the focus from anxiety-inducing uncertainties to concrete steps and accomplishments.

- Structured Routine: Incorporating journaling into a daily routine provides structure. A consistent practice can offer a sense of stability, which is particularly beneficial for those dealing with anxiety.

- Communication with Therapists or Support Networks: Journal entries can serve as valuable communication tools with mental health professionals or support networks. Sharing written reflections provides insights into one's emotional state and thought processes.

Incorporating journaling into a holistic approach to managing anxiety allows individuals to develop self-awareness, coping skills, and a sense of empowerment. It is a personal and flexible tool that can be adapted to suit individual preferences and needs.

Maintaining a journal is like having a personal companion to document your thoughts, feelings, and the situations that stir up anxiety. It's a dedicated space for self-reflection, providing a window into recurring themes that offer a deeper understanding of your unique triggers and stressors. It's a journey of discovery through the pages of your own story.

Mindfulness/Awareness Practices

Mindfulness and self-awareness practices are effective tools for managing anxiety by cultivating a present-focused, non-judgmental awareness of thoughts and feelings. Here's how these practices can be beneficial:

- Present Moment Focus: Mindfulness encourages individuals to focus on the present moment, redirecting attention away from future worries. By grounding oneself in the "here and now," anxiety about the uncertain future can be alleviated.

- Observing Thoughts Non-Judgmentally: Mindfulness involves observing thoughts without judgment. This non-critical awareness helps individuals recognize anxious thoughts without becoming overwhelmed by them. It creates a mental space to respond to thoughts more objectively.

- Acceptance of Emotions: Rather than trying to suppress or avoid anxious feelings, mindfulness encourages acceptance. Acknowledging and accepting emotions without judgment can reduce the emotional impact of anxiety.

- Breath Awareness: Mindful breathing is a common technique that involves paying attention to the breath. Focusing on the breath helps anchor individuals to the present moment, providing a simple and accessible way to manage anxiety in real-time.

- Body Scan: This technique involves mentally scanning the body to observe physical sensations. It promotes awareness of tension or discomfort related to anxiety, allowing individuals to release physical stress through relaxation.

- Cultivating Self-Compassion: Mindfulness encourages a compassionate attitude towards oneself. Self-awareness in the context of mindfulness involves recognizing and embracing one's vulnerabilities, fostering self-compassion and reducing self-critical thoughts that can contribute to anxiety.

- Interrupting Automatic Thoughts: By becoming more aware of automatic negative thoughts associated with anxiety, individuals can interrupt these thought patterns. Mindfulness helps create a space between thoughts and reactions, offering an opportunity to respond more intentionally.

- Stress Reduction: Mindfulness practices have been linked to reduced levels of the stress hormone cortisol. Regular practice can contribute to overall stress reduction, positively impacting anxiety levels.

- Increased Emotional Regulation: Mindfulness allows individuals to develop greater emotional regulation. By cultivating awareness of emotions as they arise, individuals can respond to them in a more measured and controlled manner.

- Improved Concentration: Anxiety can disrupt concentration. Mindfulness practices, including meditation and focused breathing, have been shown to enhance attention and concentration, providing individuals with a mental anchor during anxious moments.

- Enhanced Coping Skills: Mindfulness fosters resilience by helping individuals develop coping skills. The practice encourages a mindset that acknowledges difficulties without being overwhelmed, promoting adaptive responses to challenges.

Incorporating mindfulness and self-awareness practices into daily life offers a proactive and holistic approach to managing anxiety. Regular engagement with these techniques can contribute to a more balanced and resilient mindset, ultimately reducing the impact of anxiety on overall well-being.

Behavior Tracking

Behavior tracking in Cognitive Behavioral Therapy (CBT) is a practical and systematic approach that can be particularly helpful in managing anxiety. Here's how behavior tracking contributes to anxiety management within the framework of CBT:

- Identification of Patterns: Behavior tracking involves systematically recording thoughts, feelings, and behaviors related to anxiety. This process helps individuals identify recurring patterns and triggers, offering insight into the factors contributing to their anxiety.

- Increased Self-Awareness: By consistently tracking behaviors, individuals become more aware of their reactions to various situations. This heightened self-awareness is a crucial first step in understanding the relationship between thoughts, emotions, and behaviors associated with anxiety.

- Understanding Triggers: Behavior tracking allows individuals to pinpoint specific triggers that contribute to anxiety. Whether it's certain situations, thoughts, or behaviors, identifying triggers provides a foundation for developing targeted coping strategies.

- Objective Observation: Tracking behaviors provides an objective record of thoughts and actions. This objectivity helps individuals step back and observe their responses without immediate judgment, fostering a more detached and analytical perspective on their anxiety.

- Quantifiable Progress: The tracking process allows individuals to measure their progress over time. By comparing entries, individuals can observe changes in their thought patterns, emotional responses, and behaviors, providing tangible evidence of their efforts and achievements.

- Goal Setting and Reinforcement: Behavior tracking facilitates the setting of realistic goals for behavior change. Individuals can establish specific, measurable objectives to work towards, and the tracking process becomes a tool for reinforcing positive changes and achievements.

- Identifying Cognitive Distortions: CBT emphasizes recognizing and challenging cognitive distortions—irrational thought patterns that contribute to anxiety. Behavior tracking helps individuals identify and dissect these distortions, fostering a more realistic and balanced appraisal of situations.

- Intervention Planning: Armed with a detailed understanding of triggers and patterns, individuals, along with their therapists, can collaboratively develop targeted interventions. These interventions may include cognitive restructuring, exposure exercises, or the development of healthier coping mechanisms.

- Creating a Feedback Loop: Behavior tracking establishes a feedback loop between thoughts, emotions, and behaviors. This loop can be utilized to understand how changes in thoughts or behaviors impact emotional responses, allowing for more intentional and adaptive adjustments.

- Enhanced Communication with Therapist: Individuals can share their behavior tracking records with their therapists, fostering a deeper understanding of their experiences. This collaboration enables therapists to provide more targeted guidance and support, tailoring interventions to the individual's unique needs.

- Preventing Avoidance: Tracking behaviors helps individuals recognize avoidance patterns, a common response to anxiety. With this awareness, individuals can work on gradually facing feared situations or thoughts, disrupting the cycle of avoidance that can perpetuate anxiety.

In summary, behavior tracking in CBT provides a structured and evidence-based method for individuals to gain insight into their anxiety, identify patterns and triggers, set realistic goals, and collaborate with therapists to develop targeted interventions. It serves as a practical tool for fostering self-awareness and empowering individuals to actively manage and overcome anxiety.

Thought Diaries

Cognitive Behavioral Therapy (CBT) thought diaries are valuable tools in managing anxiety by providing a structured way to identify, challenge, and reframe negative thoughts. Here's how thought diaries help with anxiety:

- Identification of Negative Thoughts: Thought diaries prompt individuals to document specific situations that trigger anxiety. This process encourages the identification of automatic negative thoughts (ANTs) associated with these situations.

- Increased Self-Awareness: By consistently recording thoughts, individuals become more aware of their cognitive patterns. This heightened self-awareness is a crucial step in understanding the connection between thoughts and emotions, a central aspect of CBT.

- Analysis of Cognitive Distortions: CBT recognizes cognitive distortions—irrational thought patterns that contribute to anxiety. Thought diaries help individuals identify distortions such as catastrophizing, black-and-white thinking, and overgeneralization. Recognizing these distortions allows for more accurate assessments of situations.

- Realistic Thought Replacement: Once negative thoughts are identified, individuals work on challenging and replacing them with more realistic and balanced alternatives. Thought diaries guide individuals through the process of questioning the validity of negative thoughts and developing alternative, healthier perspectives.

- Emotion-Thought Connection: Thought diaries facilitate the exploration of the link between thoughts and emotions. Individuals can observe how specific thoughts contribute to their emotional states, enhancing their understanding of the cognitive-emotional interplay in anxiety.

- Behavioral Response Analysis: Individuals record their behavioral responses to negative thoughts in thought diaries. This includes actions taken or avoided due to anxious thoughts. Analyzing these behaviors helps identify patterns of avoidance and guides the development of more adaptive responses.

- Establishment of Evidence: Thought diaries encourage individuals to gather evidence that supports or contradicts their negative thoughts. This process helps in objectively evaluating the accuracy of their perceptions and challenging unfounded beliefs contributing to anxiety.

- Tracking Progress: Over time, individuals can review past thought diaries to observe changes in their thinking patterns and emotional responses. This reflection serves as tangible evidence of progress and reinforces the effectiveness of challenging negative thoughts.

- Goal Setting and Positive Affirmations: Thought diaries allow individuals to set goals for changing negative thought patterns. Additionally, they provide space for integrating positive affirmations or coping statements that counteract anxious thoughts, promoting a more positive mindset.

- Communication with Therapist: Individuals can share their thought diaries with their therapists during sessions. This collaboration enhances the therapeutic process, allowing therapists to gain deeper insights into the individual's cognitive processes and tailor interventions accordingly.

- Prevention of Catastrophizing: Thought diaries assist individuals in reframing catastrophic thoughts. By breaking down overwhelming situations into smaller, more manageable components, individuals can reduce the intensity of their anxiety and develop a more adaptive perspective.

In summary, CBT thought diaries serve as a practical and structured tool for individuals to identify and challenge negative thoughts, fostering increased self-awareness and promoting healthier cognitive patterns. This process is integral to anxiety management within the CBT framework, encouraging individuals to actively reshape their thinking for long-term well-being.

Anxiety Scales

Cognitive Behavioral Therapy (CBT) anxiety scales, often known as anxiety rating scales or self-monitoring tools, can be instrumental in managing anxiety. These scales provide a systematic way for individuals to track and assess their anxiety levels over time. Here's how CBT anxiety scales contribute to anxiety management:

In summary, CBT anxiety scales serve as valuable tools for individuals to measure, track, and manage their anxiety levels. They provide a structured and systematic approach to understanding and addressing anxiety within the framework of Cognitive Behavioral Therapy.

Case Studies on the Personal Impact of Anxiety

Real-life case studies from those who have faced anxiety head-on give us a glimpse into the diverse ways that anxiety manifests and affects individuals. There's more to these stories than symptoms and solutions- they bring the experience to life, making it relatable and showing us that mapping isn't just a method, it's a companion on the path to better days.

Case Study 1: Rachel's Journey to Self-Discovery

Rachel — a remarkable 28-year-old navigating the complexities of social anxiety while juggling the demands of her professional life. In her quest for growth, Rachel discovered the transformative power hidden within the pages of a simple journal and the insightful act of tracking her behaviors.

As she poured her thoughts onto paper, Rachel unearthed a common thread weaving through her experiences — a tendency to avoid social events and downplay her achievements. It was a coping mechanism, a shield she instinctively raised to guard against the perceived judgment of others.

But Rachel wasn't content with merely recognizing these patterns. Armed with newfound self-awareness, she embarked on a courageous journey of self-discovery. With each stroke of her pen, she confronted the negative thoughts that had held her captive for so long. It was a gradual process, a series of small victories that eventually paved the way for more social interactions.

Rachel's story is a testament to the incredible strength that resides within each of us. She faced the mirror of self-reflection, challenged her own narrative, and emerged stronger. Through her journey, she not only increased her social engagements but also embarked on a profound rebuilding of her self-esteem. Rachel's tale is a reminder that in the face of anxiety, the power to rewrite our stories lies within our own hearts and minds.

Case Study 2: Mark's Thought Diary Transformation

Mark – a resilient 35-year-old navigating the tumultuous waters of panic attacks, a journey that would redefine his relationship with anxiety. Armed with nothing more than thought diaries, Mark embarked on a courageous exploration, determined to unravel the enigma of his anxiety triggers.

In the quiet moments of introspection, Mark discovered something profound – a revelation hidden within the folds of his own thoughts. It was an intense fear, a fear of losing control that had silently governed his life during panic episodes.

Mark, however, was undeterred. With a steely resolve, he took charge of his narrative. Through exposure exercises that tested the boundaries of his comfort zone and the courageous act of challenging those haunting thoughts, Mark not only gained mastery over his panic attacks but, more significantly, he reclaimed a precious sense of control in the intricate tapestry of his life.

Mark's journey is more than a triumph over panic; it's a testament to the resilience of the human spirit. In confronting his fears head-on, he discovered a newfound strength and an unwavering ability to shape his own destiny. His story resonates with the indomitable spirit that resides within each of us, reminding us that, in the face of anxiety, the power to reclaim control is a journey worth taking.

These real-life stories shine a light on the remarkable impact of mapping anxiety. Through the application of mapping techniques, individuals seize control of their mental well-being, cultivating self-awareness and paving the way for tailored interventions.

As we close the chapter on behavioral techniques, let's reflect on the stories shared—the tales of Rachel and Mark, each a testament to the transformative power of facing fears and embracing positive behaviors.

Imagine behavioral activation not as a clinical term but as a friend encouraging you to step into the sunlight, bask in the joy of positive activities, and reclaim a sense of accomplishment.

Exposure therapy, the brave confrontation with fears, becomes less clinical jargon and more of a courageous journey, much like Mark's, where facing the fear of losing control led to a rediscovery of mastery.

So, as we part ways with Chapter 3, let's carry the wisdom that behavioral techniques aren't just strategies—they are companions in our quest for resilience, joy, and a life well-lived. May your journey be filled with steps taken in sunlight, facing fears, and the gentle reassurance of newfound strengths. Until the next chapter unfolds, may you navigate life's waters with courage and grace.

Cognitive Techniques for Anxiety Management

In this chapter, we're diving into the world of cognitive techniques—a key player in Cognitive Behavioral Therapy (CBT) that packs a punch when it comes to handling anxiety. Here, we're exploring the nitty-gritty of these techniques, honing in on spotting and shaking up those tricky thinking patterns, all part of the game-changing process known as cognitive restructuring.

Identifying and Challenging Distorted Thinking Patterns

In the world of cognitive techniques, we start with a simple truth – our thoughts hold immense power over how we feel and act. Anxiety usually creeps in when our minds play tricks on us with distorted thinking patterns – those automatic thoughts that tend to be a bit irrational, blown out of proportion, or just plain unrealistic. Spotting these tricky patterns is like the first step in mastering the art of anxiety management.

Common Distorted Thinking Patterns

Let's dive into some familiar ways our minds sometimes play tricks on us:

Catastrophizing

Catastrophizing is a cognitive distortion, a pattern of thought where an individual perceives a situation as far worse, more dire, or catastrophic than it actually is. It involves imagining and expecting the worst possible outcome, often in response to a relatively minor event or challenge. Catastrophizing tends to magnify the negative aspects of a situation and can contribute to increased anxiety and stress. Here are key components and characteristics of catastrophizing:

- Exaggeration of Consequences: Catastrophizing

involves an exaggerated belief that the consequences of a situation will be overwhelmingly negative. For example, a minor mistake at work may be blown out of proportion, leading to thoughts of losing one's job or damaging one's entire career.

- Anticipating the Worst-Case Scenario: Individuals engaging in catastrophizing typically focus on the worst-case scenario. They envision the most extreme and negative outcomes, even when the likelihood of such outcomes is low. This mental habit often involves imagining a chain reaction of disastrous events.

- Emotional Amplification: Catastrophizing is accompanied by a heightened emotional response. Individuals may experience intense feelings of fear, anxiety, or despair based on their catastrophic thoughts. These emotions can further cloud judgment and decision-making.

- Difficulty in Seeing Alternatives: Catastrophizing tends to narrow one's perspective, making it challenging to consider alternative, more realistic outcomes. The individual becomes fixated on the perceived catastrophic result, ignoring the possibility of less severe or positive consequences.

- Globalizing a Single Event: Catastrophizing often involves taking a single event and applying it to all aspects of life. For instance, a failed social interaction may lead to thoughts that one is universally disliked or destined for a life of loneliness.

- Impact on Coping Strategies: Individuals who engage in catastrophizing may adopt maladaptive coping strategies, such as avoidance or procrastination, in an attempt to avoid the anticipated catastrophe. This can lead to a cycle of increased stress and impaired problem-solving.

- Chronic Worry: Catastrophizing is closely related to chronic worry. Individuals may find themselves repeatedly ruminating on potential catastrophic outcomes, creating a persistent state of anxiety and unease.

- Cognitive Distortion: Catastrophizing is considered a cognitive distortion in cognitive-behavioral therapy (CBT). CBT aims to identify and challenge these distorted thought patterns to promote more realistic and balanced thinking.

Addressing catastrophizing often involves cognitive restructuring, a therapeutic technique in which individuals learn to identify, challenge, and replace negative thought patterns with more realistic and balanced ones. By becoming aware of catastrophizing tendencies and practicing alternative ways of thinking, individuals can reduce anxiety and cultivate a more adaptive mindset.

Black-and-White Thinking

Black-and-white thinking, also known as all-or-nothing thinking, is a cognitive distortion characterized by viewing situations in extremes without considering any middle ground or nuances. In the context of anxiety, black-and-white thinking can significantly contribute to heightened stress and emotional distress. Here's how black-and-white thinking manifests in anxiety:

- Extreme Evaluation of Situations: Individuals prone to black-and-white thinking tend to evaluate situations as either entirely good or completely bad, with little room for middle-ground perspectives. In anxiety, this can mean seeing potential stressors as catastrophic, without acknowledging any positive or neutral aspects.

- Polarized Emotional Responses: Black-and-white thinking amplifies emotional responses. Anxiety may be experienced as overwhelming fear or panic, while situations perceived as "safe" are met with a disproportionate sense of relief. The emotional rollercoaster intensifies due to the lack of emotional moderation.

- Catastrophizing: Black-and-white thinking often involves catastrophizing, where individuals envision the worst possible outcome in any given situation. This extreme perspective can fuel anxiety, making it challenging to approach challenges with a realistic and balanced mindset.

- Perfectionism: Black-and-white thinking is closely linked to perfectionism, where individuals set unrealistically high standards for themselves and others. In the context of anxiety, the fear of making mistakes or falling short of these standards can be paralyzing, hindering effective problem-solving.

- Rigidity in Thinking: Black-and-white thinking fosters a rigid mindset, leaving little room for flexibility or adaptation. This rigidity can exacerbate anxiety, especially when faced with uncertainties or situations that don't fit neatly into predefined categories of "good" or "bad."

- Social Interactions: In social situations, black-and-white thinking can lead to extreme evaluations of relationships. For instance, if a social interaction doesn't go perfectly, an individual might conclude that the relationship is entirely damaged. This can contribute to social anxiety and avoidance.

- Self-Evaluation: Individuals with anxiety and black-and-white thinking may apply extreme evaluations to themselves. A perceived failure or mistake may lead to self-criticism and a belief that they are entirely inadequate or unworthy.

- Binary Approach to Coping: Black-and-white thinking can limit coping strategies. Individuals may resort to all-or-nothing approaches, such as avoiding challenges altogether or demanding unrealistic guarantees of success to alleviate anxiety.

- Intolerance of Uncertainty: Black-and-white thinking is associated with an intolerance of uncertainty. The inability to tolerate ambiguity or the unknown can heighten anxiety, as situations are either seen as completely safe or dangerously threatening.

Addressing black-and-white thinking in the context of anxiety often involves cognitive-behavioral therapy (CBT). CBT aims to help individuals recognize and challenge these distorted thought patterns, fostering more balanced and flexible thinking. Developing the ability to consider shades of gray in various situations can contribute to a more adaptive and less anxiety-driven mindset.

Mind Reading

Mind-reading, in the context of cognitive distortions, refers to the tendency to believe that we know what others are thinking or how they perceive us, even when there is little or no evidence to support such assumptions. This cognitive distortion can have a significant impact on anxiety. Here's how mind-reading and anxiety are interconnected:

- Assumption of Negative Thoughts: Mind-reading often involves assuming that others are thinking negatively about us. In social situations, individuals with anxiety may believe that they are being judged, criticized, or disliked by others, even in the absence of clear evidence. This assumption of negative thoughts can fuel anxiety and self-consciousness.

- Heightened Sensitivity to Social Cues: Those prone to mind-reading may be hyper-vigilant to social cues, interpreting ambiguous or neutral behavior as confirmation of negative thoughts. For example, if someone doesn't smile or makes a neutral facial expression, the individual may automatically assume that the other person dislikes them, contributing to heightened anxiety in social interactions.

- Anticipation of Rejection: Mind-reading often involves anticipating rejection or disapproval from others. Individuals with anxiety may preoccupy themselves with thoughts of being unworthy, unlikable, or a burden to others, leading to increased anxiety, self-doubt, and fear of social interactions.

- Impact on Self-Esteem: Continuous mind-reading can erode self-esteem. The assumed negative thoughts of others may contribute to feelings of inadequacy and a distorted self-perception, intensifying anxiety and creating a self-fulfilling prophecy where the fear of judgment becomes a barrier to positive social experiences.

- Avoidance Behaviors: The anxiety stemming from mind-reading can lead to avoidance behaviors. Individuals may avoid social situations, refrain from expressing their opinions, or withdraw from interactions altogether to protect themselves from the perceived negative thoughts of others. These avoidance behaviors can, in turn, reinforce social anxiety.

- Interpersonal Relationships: In relationships, mind-reading can create misunderstandings and conflict. Assuming the thoughts and intentions of others without clear communication can lead to strained relationships, as the person may react defensively or withdraw based on unfounded assumptions.

- Negative Self-Talk: Mind-reading often accompanies negative self-talk. Internal dialogue that reinforces the belief that others hold negative opinions can contribute to a negative mindset, further exacerbating anxiety and decreasing overall well-being.

Addressing the relationship between mind-reading and anxiety often involves cognitive-behavioral therapy (CBT). CBT aims to help individuals recognize and challenge distorted thought patterns, including mind-reading, by encouraging more balanced and evidence-based thinking. Developing effective communication skills and building self-confidence are also important components in mitigating the impact of mind-reading on anxiety.

Filtering

Filtering is a cognitive distortion that involves selectively focusing on certain aspects of a situation while ignoring or minimizing others. This distorted thinking pattern can contribute to anxiety by shaping how individuals perceive and interpret events. Here's how the relationship between filtering and anxiety unfolds:

- Selective Attention to Negatives: Filtering involves concentrating on negative aspects of a situation while filtering out positive or neutral elements. In the context of anxiety, individuals may disproportionately focus on potential threats, risks, or negative outcomes, heightening their overall sense of worry and unease.

- Magnification of Problems: Filtering tends to magnify problems, making them appear more significant and insurmountable than they actually are. In anxiety, individuals may amplify the negative implications of a situation, contributing to feelings of overwhelm and a sense of helplessness.

- Overlooking Positives: Individuals who engage in filtering may overlook positive aspects of a situation or evidence that contradicts their negative perceptions. This can lead to a skewed and unbalanced view of reality, reinforcing anxious thoughts and feelings.

- Perfectionism: Filtering is often associated with perfectionism, where individuals set unrealistically high standards for themselves. In anxiety, this perfectionistic tendency may lead to a constant focus on perceived flaws, mistakes, or shortcomings, intensifying feelings of stress and anxiety.

- Confirmation Bias: Filtering is related to confirmation bias, the tendency to seek, interpret, and remember information that confirms existing beliefs. In anxiety, individuals may actively look for evidence that supports their anxious thoughts, disregarding information that contradicts these negative perceptions.

- Cognitive Rigidity: Filtering contributes to cognitive rigidity, limiting individuals' ability to consider alternative perspectives or interpretations. This inflexibility can lead to persistent anxious thoughts, as individuals may feel stuck in a narrow, negative frame of mind.

- Negative Self-Talk: Filtering often accompanies negative self-talk, where individuals use harsh and critical language to describe themselves or their circumstances. This negative internal dialogue reinforces anxious thoughts, contributing to a cycle of heightened anxiety.

- Impact on Decision-Making: Filtering can impact decision-making by causing individuals to focus excessively on potential negative outcomes or risks. This heightened focus on negatives may lead to hesitancy, avoidance, or reluctance to take reasonable risks, hindering personal and professional growth.

Addressing the relationship between filtering and anxiety typically involves cognitive-behavioral therapy (CBT). CBT aims to help individuals recognize and challenge distorted thought patterns, including filtering, by encouraging a more balanced and realistic evaluation of situations. Developing cognitive flexibility and adopting a more constructive and positive mindset are key components of mitigating the impact of filtering on anxiety.

Personalization

Personalization, as a cognitive distortion, involves attributing external events to oneself without reasonable evidence. In the context of anxiety, personalization often leads individuals to take undue responsibility for events, situations, or outcomes, contributing to heightened stress and anxious feelings. Here's how the relationship between personalization and anxiety unfolds:

- Excessive Self-Blame: Personalization often involves an exaggerated sense of personal responsibility for negative events. In anxiety, individuals may automatically assume that they are to blame for things going wrong, even when the events are beyond their control. This excessive self-blame can fuel feelings of guilt and anxiety.

- Magnification of Impact: Personalization tends to magnify one's perceived impact on events. Individuals with anxiety may believe that their actions or presence significantly influence outcomes, leading to an inflated sense of responsibility. This magnification can contribute to heightened stress and worry about potential negative consequences.

- Heightened Sensitivity to Rejection: Personalization can make individuals highly sensitive to perceived rejection or criticism. They may internalize external events, such as a colleague's criticism or a friend's distant behavior, interpreting them as direct reflections of their own inadequacy or flaws. This sensitivity can intensify social anxiety and feelings of rejection.

- Constant Self-Scrutiny: Individuals engaging in personalization often engage in constant self-scrutiny, examining their own behavior and actions for any potential flaws or mistakes. This self-focused scrutiny can lead to heightened self-consciousness, anxiety about social interactions, and a persistent fear of being negatively judged by others.

- Cognitive Distortion: Personalization is considered a cognitive distortion in cognitive-behavioral therapy (CBT). It involves a distorted way of thinking that contributes to emotional distress. CBT aims to help individuals identify and challenge such distortions, fostering more balanced and realistic thinking patterns.

- Impact on Self-Esteem: The constant attribution of events to oneself can erode self-esteem. Individuals may develop a negative self-image, feeling as though they are a burden or that their actions are constantly under scrutiny. This negative self-perception can contribute to chronic anxiety.

- Avoidance Behaviors: Personalization can lead to avoidance behaviors, as individuals may fear making mistakes or causing negative outcomes. This fear of being responsible for negative consequences can result in avoidance of challenges, opportunities, or social interactions, limiting personal growth and reinforcing anxiety.

- Interpersonal Relationships: Personalization can impact interpersonal relationships by creating a heightened sense of responsibility for the dynamics within relationships. Individuals may carry an undue burden for conflicts or misunderstandings, leading to strained relationships and increased anxiety in social settings.

Addressing the relationship between personalization and anxiety often involves therapeutic interventions, particularly cognitive-behavioral therapy. CBT helps individuals recognize and challenge distorted thought patterns, fostering more realistic and balanced perspectives. Developing skills to accurately assess one's level of responsibility in various situations is crucial for reducing anxiety associated with personalization.

These thinking habits are part of being human, and we all have our moments. The key is recognizing them, because understanding is the first step toward rewiring our thought patterns. We're all in this together, navigating the twists and turns of our minds!

Cognitive Restructuring to Develop More Balanced Thinking

Cognitive restructuring is like giving your thoughts a makeover – we're talking about challenging those sneaky distorted thoughts and turning them into a more balanced and down-to-earth perspective. It's a bit like being your own detective, digging into the evidence for and against those automatic thoughts, spotting the mind's little tricks, and coming up with alternative, more sensible interpretations. It's basically helping your mind see things from a fresher and clearer point of view.

Steps in Cognitive Restructuring

Embarking on the journey of cognitive restructuring is like giving your mind a much-needed makeover, shedding the weight of anxiety-triggering thoughts. Let's break down the steps in a more human and relatable way:

Spot the Sneaky Thought

Begin by playing the role of a mental detective. Imagine catching that sneaky thought, the troublemaker behind your anxiety, red-handed. Picture it like unmasking a mischievous gremlin, revealing its true nature.

Challenge the Intruder

Channel your inner detective skills and question the evidence behind the thought. Is it standing on solid ground, rooted in facts, or is it merely floating on a cloud of assumptions? Sometimes, thoughts need a reality check, like putting the mischievous gremlin on trial.

Swap for Something Better

Now, it's time for a brainstorming session. Picture yourself revamping your mind's wardrobe. Replace those outdated, anxiety-inducing thought styles with fresh and trendy alternatives. It's like decluttering your mental closet and choosing thoughts that spark joy.

Evaluate the New Look

Stand in front of the mental mirror and check out your new thoughts. How do they hold up? Assess the validity of these upgraded interpretations and feel the impact they have on your mental state. It's all about finding the thoughts that not only look good but make your mind feel good.

In this journey of cognitive restructuring, you're not just tackling thoughts; you're giving your mind a makeover, embracing styles that empower rather than weigh you down. It's a process of self-discovery and transformation, turning your mental space into a sanctuary of positivity and resilience.

Cognitive restructuring is your mental glow-up – a process of shedding the old and embracing a new, more positive outlook. It's like decluttering your mental closet and making space for thoughts that bring joy and resilience. Remember, Rome wasn't built in a day, and neither is a **brand-new** mindset. It's a journey, and you're the designer of your mental landscape!

Homework Exercises to Practice Cognitive Techniques

Mastering cognitive techniques is a bit like learning to ride a bike – it takes practice to get the hang of it. So, let's treat it like a mental workout, your personal training ground to flex those cognitive muscles and build resilience against the anxiety that tends to sneak up on us. Here are some exercises to kickstart your cognitive journey:

Thought Diaries

Think of these as your mental journaling sessions. Jot down those automatic thoughts, unravel the emotions they bring, and explore alternative interpretations. It's like mapping out the terrain of your mind, discovering hidden paths to navigate through anxious moments.

Daily Monitoring

Consider this your daily check-in. Keep a log of your activities, thoughts, and the emotions tagging along. It's like creating a roadmap of your day, helping you spot patterns and understand how your thoughts influence your emotional landscape.

Role-Playing

Imagine this as a rehearsal for life's little dramas. Simulate scenarios that usually trigger anxiety and practice cognitive restructuring. It's like having a dress rehearsal for the mind, preparing yourself to face real-life situations with a newfound sense of calm and control.

Homework exercises aren't just tasks; they're your safe playground to apply these cognitive techniques. It's about gradually building confidence in your ability to manage those sneaky anxiety-inducing thoughts that often pop up when we least expect them.As we conclude this chapter, we find ourselves at the crossroads of understanding distorted thinking patterns. The stories we've explored are not detached narratives but windows into the human experience—journeys through the twists and turns of the mind.

Consider the familiar companions of catastrophizing, black-and-white thinking, mind reading, filtering, and personalization. These are not just terms; they are echoes of the mental landscapes we navigate daily.

As we bid adieu to this chapter, let's carry with us the awareness that cognitive restructuring isn't just a therapeutic technique; it's an invitation to dance with our thoughts. It's about breaking free from the shackles of negativity, upgrading our mental software, and embracing a more realistic outlook.

So, until the next chapter unfolds, let's continue this dance, step by step, reshaping our cognitive landscapes and finding the melody within our minds. May your thoughts be harmonious, your perspectives balanced, and your journey through the labyrinth of the mind be one of discovery and resilience.

Behavioral Techniques for Anxiety Relief

Consider behavioral techniques as your personal compass for navigating the realms of anxiety.

Facing Fears: Exposure Therapy Explained

Leading the way is exposure therapy, a bit like embarking on an adventurous journey through your fears. It involves deliberately confronting anxiety-triggering situations or stimuli, carefully pacing yourself through each challenge. Think of it as embarking on a quest where, with each step, you're working towards desensitizing yourself to fears and cultivating a more adaptive response over time. It's a journey of self-discovery and resilience-building, with exposure therapy as your guide through uncharted territories of anxiety.

Principles of Exposure Therapy

The principles of exposure therapy are as follows:

- Systematic Desensitization: Exposure is systematically structured, starting with less anxiety-inducing elements and progressing to more challenging aspects as individuals build tolerance.

- Flooding: In some cases, individuals may be exposed to the most feared situations immediately, flooding their senses with the feared stimuli. This accelerated approach aims to diminish anxiety through prolonged exposure.

- Cognitive Restructuring: Concurrently, cognitive techniques may be employed to challenge and reframe negative thoughts associated with the feared situations.

Imagine exposure therapy as your trusty sidekick on the road to conquering anxiety. It's like a versatile tool that proves its worth in various scenarios, from facing phobias to tackling panic attacks and navigating the aftermath of traumatic experiences like a true companion. So, when it comes to your anxiety battles, exposure therapy is the ally you can rely on for diverse challenges, ready to support you through the ups and downs of your mental health journey.

Behavioral Activation to Combat Avoidance

Think of behavioral activation as your personal cheerleader, nudging you to step into the arena of positive actions, even when anxiety or low spirits try to keep you on the sidelines. It's like having a friendly coach guiding you through a game plan to break free from the grip of avoidance. By encouraging you to participate in activities that bring joy and a sense of accomplishment, behavioral activation becomes your trusted ally in the quest for mental well-being, reminding you that even small steps can lead to significant victories.

Key Components of Behavioral Activation

The key components of behavioral activation include:

- Activity Monitoring: Individuals keep a log of their daily activities, mood levels, and the presence of any avoidance behaviors.

- Activity Scheduling: Therapists and individuals collaboratively plan and schedule enjoyable and meaningful activities, aiming to increase positive reinforcement and counteract avoidance.

- Graded Task Assignment: Gradual exposure to avoided activities, encouraging individuals to face anxiety-provoking situations in a structured manner.

Imagine behavioral activation as your personal life-enhancer, guiding you to sprinkle positivity and fulfillment back into your daily routine. It's like rekindling the joy of activities that resonate with your true self. Step by step, as you reintroduce these positive experiences, you're not just breaking free from the chains of avoidance – you're creating a symphony of accomplishment and joy that plays in the background of your life. It's a journey where every small victory adds a note to the melody of your well-being.

Relaxation and Stress Reduction Methods

In addition to exposure therapy and behavioral activation, relaxation/stress reduction methods are critical for overall anxiety relief. These techniques are designed to counteract the physiological signs of anxiety.

Common Relaxation Techniques

Several relaxation techniques have proven effective in combating anxiety. Here are some common ones:

Deep Breathing Exercises

- Description: Inhale deeply through your nose, expanding your diaphragm, hold for a moment, and then exhale slowly through pursed lips.

- Effect: Calms the nervous system, reduces tension, and promotes mindfulness.

Progressive Muscle Relaxation (PMR)

- Description: Tense and then gradually release each muscle group, starting from your toes and working your way up to your head.

- Effect: Releases physical tension and promotes a sense of relaxation.

Mindfulness Meditation

- Description: Focus on your breath or present

sensations without judgment, bringing your attention back when it wanders.

- Effect: Enhances awareness, reduces stress, and cultivates a sense of presence.

Guided Imagery

- Description: Imagine a peaceful scene or engage in a guided visualization, focusing on sensory details.

- Effect: Redirects your mind, creating a mental escape and promoting relaxation.

Yoga

- Description: Combines physical postures, breath control, and meditation.

- Effect: Enhances flexibility, reduces stress, and promotes a sense of well-being.

Autogenic Training

- Description: Repeat a series of visualizations and affirmations to promote a sense of warmth and heaviness in different parts of your body.

- Effect: Induces a state of relaxation and calm.

Aromatherapy

- Description: Use scents like lavender, chamomile, or eucalyptus through essential oils, candles, or diffusers.

- Effect: Engages the sense of smell, promoting relaxation and reducing stress.

Tai Chi

- Description: A gentle, flowing sequence of movements combined with deep breathing.

- Effect: Enhances physical and mental well-being and reduces anxiety.

Listening to Music

- Description: Choose calming music and listen mindfully.

- Effect: Alters mood and reduces stress hormone levels.

Journaling

- Description: Write down your thoughts, feelings, and worries.

- Effect: Provides a cathartic release, helps organize thoughts, and fosters self-reflection.

It's important to explore different techniques and find what works best for you. Integrating these practices into your routine can contribute to a more relaxed and balanced life. These techniques not only provide immediate relief from heightened anxiety but also contribute to long-term resilience and coping skills.

As we close the pages of this chapter, we bid farewell to the exploration of mindfulness techniques—a journey that unfolded like a heartfelt conversation with an old friend.

As we step away from these pages, let's carry the essence of mindfulness with us—a tool for not just managing anxiety but embracing the richness of each present moment. The journey continues, promising more insights, more stories, and more tools for navigating the labyrinth of the mind.

So, until the next chapter beckons, let the echoes of mindfulness resonate within, fostering a sanctuary of calm amidst life's storms. May your journey be filled with self-discovery, and may each breath be a step towards a more mindful, grounded existence.

Advanced CBT Strategies

Advanced Cognitive Behavioral Therapy strategies provide us with a sophisticated toolkit for managing anxiety. In this chapter, we will explore the following advanced CBT strategies: problem-solving techniques, assertiveness and communication skills, and mindfulness-based cognitive therapy.

Problem-Solving Techniques for Dealing with Anxiety-Inducing Situations

In the world of Cognitive Behavioral Therapy, problem-solving techniques emerge as a valuable ally, providing individuals with a structured and practical approach to untangle and resolve stressors that contribute to anxiety. Picture it as a roadmap, guiding individuals through the twists and turns of life's challenges with a clear strategy for navigating the complexities.

At its core, problem-solving within CBT is like having a trustworthy companion by your side, ready to help you face the issues that fuel your anxiety. It involves breaking down problems into manageable parts, exploring potential solutions, and weighing the pros and cons of each option. It's not just about finding any solution but discovering the one that aligns with your values and goals – a tailored approach to problem-solving that feels uniquely yours.

Consider problem-solving techniques as a toolkit filled with practical instruments. It encourages brainstorming, inviting you to explore creative solutions, fostering a sense of autonomy and control. It's not about imposing rigid formulas but adapting strategies to fit the contours of your specific situation, acknowledging the uniqueness of your journey.

The beauty of problem-solving within CBT lies in its flexibility. It's not a one-size-fits-all prescription; instead, it's a personalized guide crafted to match your needs. As you engage with these techniques, it becomes a dynamic process, an ongoing dialogue between you and the challenges you face. You're not just solving problems; you're cultivating a skill – a skill that empowers you to face future hurdles with confidence.

In essence, problem-solving techniques in CBT are more than just a set of steps; they're a narrative woven into the fabric of your journey. They're an invitation to navigate the twists and turns of life's challenges, armed with a personalized roadmap that resonates with your values, strengths, and aspirations.

Steps in Problem-Solving Techniques

Let's break down this problem-solving journey into more relatable terms:

Identifying the Issue

Picture this as shining a light on what's bothering you. It's like putting words to that thing that keeps nagging at you, defining the problem so you can get a good look at it.

Setting Goals

Imagine you're setting out on a road trip. You don't just aimlessly drive; you decide on your destination. Similarly, setting goals means figuring out where you want to go and breaking it down into smaller, doable steps.

Coming Up with Ideas

Think of this as a brainstorming session with yourself or others. Imagine a creativity session where you let ideas flow without judging them. It's about exploring all the possibilities, even the seemingly wild ones.

Weighing Your Options

Now, you're like a detective weighing the evidence. What are the pros and cons of each idea? What could happen if you go down a particular path? It's all about considering the good and the not-so-good.

Making a Choice

Picture standing at a crossroads and deciding which path to take. Choosing the best solution involves considering your values, priorities, and what you have to work with – like picking the route that aligns with your personal map.

Putting Your Plan into Action

Now you're like a project manager bringing your plan to life. It's not just about deciding; it's about doing. You create a roadmap, start taking steps, and keep an eye on how things are unfolding.

See, problem-solving is a bit like navigating through life with a compass. It's about understanding where you are, figuring out where you want to go, exploring all the routes, making a thoughtful choice, and then taking steps with confidence. And just like any journey, you might need to adjust your route along the way. It's all part of the adventure!

By learning and applying these problem-solving techniques, we create a structured approach to navigating anxiety-inducing situations, promoting a sense of control and efficacy.

Assertiveness and Communication Skills to Reduce Social Anxiety

Imagine stepping into a room and feeling like all eyes are on you, and not in a good way. Social anxiety can be like having this constant fear of being judged or rejected in social situations. Now, let's dive into some savvy CBT strategies that go beyond the basics.

Think of it as a toolkit for boosting your social confidence:

Assertiveness Training

Ever wish you could express yourself more confidently? Assertiveness training is like a crash course in speaking up without feeling anxious or overly submissive. It's about finding that sweet spot where you're respectful but firm in expressing your thoughts and needs.

Communication Skills Refinement

Imagine refining your communication skills as if you're upgrading your social navigation system. This involves learning the art of effective listening, understanding non-verbal cues, and expressing yourself clearly. It's like enhancing your ability to steer through conversations with ease.

Confidence Building

Picture a confidence boost as adding some extra fuel to your social engine. CBT strategies focus on building your self-esteem and confidence so that social interactions become more like opportunities to shine rather than sources of anxiety.

Exposure to Social Situations

It's like taking small, manageable steps toward facing your social fears. Exposure therapy in CBT gently guides you to gradually engage in social situations, helping you become more comfortable and less anxious over time.

So, think of advanced CBT for social anxiety as your personalized social superhero training. It's about equipping you with the skills and mindset to step into social scenes not as a nervous participant but as a confident, authentic you.

Key Components of Assertiveness Training

Let's break down the nuts and bolts of assertiveness training in a way that feels more like a friendly chat than a workshop manual.

Self-Expression

It's all about letting your thoughts, feelings, and needs out into the open. Imagine it as unlocking a treasure chest of your genuine self and sharing it with the world. Assertiveness training is like giving you the tools to express yourself openly and honestly, without the fear of being misunderstood.

Setting Boundaries

Picture this as drawing a line in the sand but in a friendly, respectful way. Assertiveness training encourages you to establish and communicate your personal boundaries. It's about letting others know what's okay and what's not, creating a space where you feel comfortable and respected.

Active Listening

Think of it as turning up the volume on your social radar. Assertiveness training hones your ability to listen attentively and respond with empathy. It's like tuning into others' wavelengths, making social interactions more meaningful and connected.

Effective Communication

Imagine having a superpower that makes your thoughts and feelings crystal clear. Assertiveness training is like developing this power. It helps you communicate assertively, expressing yourself in a way that's both clear and concise. No more fumbling for the right words or feeling unheard.

By embracing assertiveness and communication skills, social interactions become less like a tightrope walk and more like a dance. It's about turning those moments into opportunities for genuine connection and self-expression, without the looming cloud of anxiety.

Mindfulness-Based Cognitive Therapy

Mindfulness-Based Cognitive Therapy (MBCT) is like blending the best of two worlds – traditional problem-solving with a sprinkle of mindfulness magic. It's designed for folks who've dealt with depression or long-lasting anxiety more than once.

Here's the breakdown:

Traditional Problem-Solving

You know how you tackle problems – thinking through them, finding solutions, and all that jazz. MBCT keeps that part intact. It's like having a reliable toolbox filled with strategies to deal with life's challenges.

Mindfulness Magic

Now, imagine adding a dash of mindfulness – the art of being fully present and aware in the moment. It's like having a superpower that helps you see your thoughts and feelings without getting too tangled up in them. A bit like stepping back to get a clearer picture.

Teaming Up for Good

MBCT brings these two approaches together like a dynamic duo. It's not about just solving problems; it's about doing it mindfully. This combo helps folks who've faced depression or ongoing anxiety learn to navigate their thoughts and emotions more skillfully.

Keeping Relapse at Bay

And the big goal? Preventing a comeback of those tough times. By learning this mindful problem-solving approach, individuals become better equipped to handle the twists and turns, reducing the chances of falling back into the same old patterns.

So, think of MBCT as your trusty sidekick in the journey of mental well-being – a blend of good problem-solving strategies and a touch of mindfulness magic to keep you on track and feeling more in control.

Key Components of MBCT

Let's take a closer look at how MBCT works:

Mindfulness Meditation

So, picture this like a mental workout, but a chill one. You practice being fully present in the moment through meditation. It's like giving your mind a little vacation from the constant buzz.

Cognitive Restructuring

This is about blending mindfulness with your thoughts. Instead of judging them, it's like observing them with a curious mindset. Think of it as having a mental balcony where you watch your thoughts go by without getting caught up in the drama.

Body Scan

Now, this is like a friendly check-in with your body. You pay attention to how it's feeling – any tension, relaxation, or random sensations. It's like saying, "Hey body, how are you doing today?"

Breath Awareness

Imagine your breath as a chill guide, keeping you grounded. You focus on your breath, and it's like a little anchor that helps you stay calm and relaxed. It's all about taking a breather, quite literally.

MBCT is like your mental superhero cape against those negative thoughts that sneak in. By practicing these techniques, you build a kind of mental shield. It helps you step back from the chaos in your head, making it less likely for those gloomy thoughts to take over.

So, MBCT is like your personal guide to a more relaxed mind – a mix of meditation, mindful thinking, body check-ins, and deep breaths to help you break free from those tricky thought patterns.

As we conclude this chapter, we stand at the crossroads where understanding intersects with action, and theory melds with practice. The landscape of cognitive restructuring and behavioral techniques unfolds before us, revealing a path paved with self-awareness and resilience.

As we bid farewell to this chapter, let it resonate as more than the end of a section—it's a prelude to empowered living. The journey toward well-being is a continuous expedition, and each insight gained, each distorted thought challenged, propels us forward.

The next chapter awaits, promising a deeper dive into advanced strategies and the fusion of mindfulness with cognitive techniques. So, let's carry the torch of self-discovery into the uncharted territories that lie ahead, where resilience becomes a guiding star and understanding transforms into enduring well-being.

Overcoming Obstacles in CBT

While CBT is a highly effective approach for managing and overcoming anxiety, there are several obstacles you may face.

Common Challenges/Barriers in Applying CBT Techniques

The most common challenges/barriers in the application of CBT in anxiety relief include the following. In order to successfully navigate the therapeutic journey effectively, we must understand these challenges.

Resistance to Change

Imagine cozying up in your favorite worn-out sweater. Change can be a bit like swapping it for something new. Some individuals find solace in their well-practiced thought patterns, even if they cause distress. It's like trading the old sweater for a newer, less familiar one – it might be comfier, but it takes some getting used to.

Lack of Insight

Think of self-awareness as wiping away the fog on a mirror. Sometimes, it's crystal clear, and you can spot every detail. Other times, it's a bit hazy, making it tricky to identify those sneaky distorted thoughts. Like peering into the mirror on a misty morning, gaining clarity takes time and patience.

Overwhelmed by Emotions

Picture navigating cognitive techniques during therapy like steering a ship through stormy seas. Emotions can be turbulent waves that challenge the journey. It's not always smooth sailing, especially when facing exposure therapy or challenging automatic thoughts. The key is to ride those emotional waves, knowing that calmer seas lie ahead.

Unrealistic Expectations

Imagine waiting for a garden to bloom – therapeutic progress is a bit like that. Some individuals might expect instant blossoms, but growth takes time. It's not about overnight transformations but rather the gradual unfurling of petals. Like tending to a garden, therapy involves cultivating patience and allowing change to unfold naturally.

These challenges are the twists and turns in the narrative of personal growth. Each hurdle offers an opportunity for learning, resilience, and a deeper understanding of oneself. It's not always a straightforward journey, but the richness lies in the complexity of the human experience.

Strategies for Overcoming Resistance and Procrastination

Addressing resistance and procrastination within the CBT landscape is akin to preparing for a challenging hike. Let's lace up our boots and explore the strategies that make the journey more manageable and rewarding:

Building Trust, One Step at a Time

Picture CBT as a shared trail, therapists and individuals side by side. The more solid the ground beneath, the easier the climb. Establishing rapport is like finding that common ground – it's the sturdy path that makes the uphill battles less daunting.

The Guidebook of Understanding

Imagine CBT as a fascinating but unfamiliar terrain. Psychoeducation acts as the guidebook, unlocking the mysteries and providing a clear map. Understanding the rationale behind CBT techniques is like decoding the landscape, making the journey more intriguing and less intimidating.

Stepping Stones of Manageability

Confronting anxiety can feel like facing a massive mountain. Breaking tasks into smaller steps is akin to placing stepping stones along the way. It transforms an overwhelming ascent into a series of manageable strides, making the journey less daunting and more achievable.

Co-Creating the Expedition Plan

Envision CBT as a joint expedition. Therapists and individuals collaboratively chart the course, much like co-creating a map. Involving individuals in goal setting is like giving them the compass – it sparks motivation and ensures active participation in the expedition towards well-being.

In the landscape of personal growth, these strategies serve as sturdy walking sticks, making the journey smoother and more enjoyable. They are not just tools; they're companions on the path to resilience and transformative change.

Maintaining Motivation and Dealing with Setbacks

Embarking on a journey through therapy is akin to setting sail on the sometimes tumultuous sea of self-discovery. To keep the sails full and navigate the waves effectively, we need strategies that resonate with the ebb and flow of motivation.

Goals as Beacons in the Night

Imagine therapeutic goals as guiding stars on the horizon. Regularly reassessing them is like checking our course under the night sky. It allows us to adjust sails based on the winds of progress and the changing currents of personal needs.

Savoring the Sweetness of Small Victories

Think of therapy as a treasure hunt, and every small achievement as a precious gem. Celebrating these wins isn't just acknowledgment; it's like collecting and admiring the treasures we find along the way. It fuels motivation and provides a sense of accomplishment.

Setbacks as Plot Twists, Not Dead Ends

Picture the therapeutic journey as a gripping novel. Setbacks are unexpected plot twists, not dead ends. Normalizing setbacks is like acknowledging that even the most thrilling stories have moments of tension and challenge. They become turning points rather than roadblocks.

The Tapestry of Success Stories

Envision a therapy room adorned with a tapestry of success stories. Revisiting these tales of triumph is like surrounding ourselves with an album of cherished memories. It's a reminder that positive change is not just possible but has been achieved before, instilling hope and resilience during challenging times.

In the grand narrative of therapy, these strategies are the compass, the treasure map, the unexpected twists, and the collection of victories—a dynamic interplay that transforms the journey into an adventure of self-discovery and growth.

As we conclude this chapter, we find ourselves on the shores of self-discovery, having explored the intricacies of anxiety and the transformative tools within our grasp. From the personalized maps drawn through journaling to the courageous exposure exercises, we've witnessed the human spirit in its quest for resilience.

As we part ways with this chapter, let it serve as a mere pause in the continuous evolution of our understanding. The journey through self-discovery is ongoing, with each page turned and every new technique embraced marking a step toward lasting well-being.

The adventure continues, and the next chapter beckons—an exploration of advanced strategies, the integration of mindfulness, and the myriad ways individuals navigate the intricate waters of their minds. May the forthcoming pages illuminate the path to resilience, growth, and enduring mental wellness.

CBT in Daily Life

The true effectiveness of CBT lies in the seamless integration into daily life. In this chapter, we will explore practical ways that we can incorporate the techniques found in this book into our everyday routine, ensuring perpetual mental health maintenance.

Tips for Integrating CBT Techniques into Everyday Routines

Let's explore a few of the ways that you can easily incorporate CBT into your daily life:

Morning Mindset Reset

Start your day with a mini-check-in. Any worries creeping in? Toss them out and set the tone for positivity. Your day, your rules!

Journaling Journey

Grab a journal, spill your thoughts, no judgment! It's like venting to your diary BFF. Plus, discover trends and craft your own "Aha!" moments.

Mindful Moments

No need for mountaintop meditation. Try mindfulness in everyday chaos. Breathe through your commute or savor each bite at meals. Your daily routine just got a zen makeover.

Thought Time-Outs

Hit pause, peek into your thoughts. Spotted negativity? Time for a cognitive revamp. Upgrade your mental software and let the positivity flow!

As you can see, it's easy to incorporate CBT techniques into your daily life, creating a happier, healthier mind.

Using CBT to Handle Acute Anxiety Attacks

When anxiety hits, it's important to have a way to manage it. CBT provides us with the tools we need to manage acute anxiety attacks in real-time. By employing the following techniques during moments of heightened anxiety, we can regain control of our mental state.

Grounding Techniques

Grounding is a set of techniques designed to anchor you in the present moment. When anxiety or stress sends your mind on a wild journey, grounding helps you reconnect with reality. It's like hitting pause on the mental chaos and tuning in to what's happening around you.

Grounding involves engaging your senses to shift your focus from overwhelming thoughts to the immediate environment. By paying close attention to what you see, hear, smell, taste, and touch, you create a sensory checkpoint that grounds you in the present.

Common Grounding Techniques

- 5-4-3-2-1 Method: Identify and name 5 things you see, 4 things you can touch, 3 things you hear, 2 things you can smell, and 1 thing you can taste.

- Sensory Awareness: Close your eyes and focus on each of your senses. What do you feel, hear, smell, taste, and see in the moment?

- Breath Focus: Pay attention to your breath. Feel the sensation of each inhale and exhale, grounding yourself in the rhythmic flow.

- Object Exploration: Take a random object and explore it with your senses. What does it feel like? Any sound it makes? What's its scent?

Grounding is like a mental reset button, helping you find stability amid life's twists and turns. It's a simple yet powerful way to reclaim control and find calm in the midst of chaos.

ABC Model

The ABC Model of CBT is a roadmap to understanding and reshaping your thought patterns. Here's how it works:

A - Activating Event

Think of A as the trigger point, the starting line of your emotional journey. It's the event or situation that sets things in motion. It could be a challenging work task, a social interaction, or even a passing comment.

B - Beliefs

Now, we delve into your beliefs or thoughts about the activating event. What interpretations or judgments are you attaching to it? These beliefs are crucial because they influence your emotional and behavioral reactions. Are you thinking it's a catastrophe, or just a minor hiccup?

C - Consequences

The aftermath – that's what C is all about. Your beliefs about the activating event lead to emotional and behavioral consequences. If you believe a situation is a disaster, you might feel anxious, upset, or frustrated (emotional consequences). These emotions, in turn, shape how you behave or react to the situation (behavioral consequences).

Let's say you made a mistake at work (Activating Event). If your belief is, "I'm a failure; I'll never get anything right" (Beliefs), you might feel demoralized and avoid taking on new tasks (Emotional and Behavioral Consequences).

The ABC Model helps you recognize that it's not the activating event alone but your beliefs about it that drive your emotional and behavioral responses. By identifying and challenging unhelpful beliefs, you can reshape your reactions and cultivate a more balanced perspective.

With the ABC Model, you gain insight into your mental processes, empowering you to navigate challenges with a clearer mindset. It's like having a decoder for your thoughts, revealing the connections between events, beliefs, and your emotional world.

Progressive Muscle Relaxation

Progressive Muscle Relaxation, or PMR, is a method for releasing physical tension and promoting relaxation. Here's how it works:

- Muscle Tension: You start by tensing a specific muscle group—say, your shoulders or fists. Hold that tension for a few seconds, like you're flexing those muscles to lift something heavy.

- Release the Tension: Now, let it all go. Picture the tension flowing out of your muscles as you release. It's like the sensation when you finally put down that heavy load—total relief.

- Repeat the Process: Move on to the next muscle group, maybe your neck or thighs. Rinse and repeat. It's like a gentle wave of relaxation washing over your body.

Why Does it Work?

Our bodies and minds are a tag team. When your muscles are tense, it sends signals to your brain that something might be off. By deliberately relaxing those muscles, you're sending a different message – "All is calm."

Benefits of PMR

PMR offers several benefits, including:

- Stress Reduction: PMR is a stress-busting powerhouse. By systematically releasing muscle tension, it sends signals to your brain that it's time to relax, helping to reduce overall stress levels.

- Improved Sleep: If you struggle with falling asleep, PMR can be your bedtime buddy. The relaxation it induces can pave the way for a more peaceful and restful night's sleep.

- Muscle Relaxation: As the name suggests, PMR is all about relaxation. It's like a massage for your muscles without the need for a spa appointment. Relaxed muscles contribute to a sense of ease in the body.

- Anxiety Management: Tension often accompanies anxiety. PMR provides a practical technique to counteract this tension, contributing to the management of anxiety symptoms.

- Mind-Body Connection: PMR encourages awareness of the mind-body connection. By consciously focusing on and relaxing each muscle group, you're fostering a deeper understanding of how mental and physical states are intertwined.

- Improved Mood: Relaxing your muscles can have a ripple effect on your mood. When your body feels at ease, it sends positive signals to your brain, contributing to an improved overall mood.

- Reduced Physical Symptoms of Stress: Stress can manifest physically, leading to headaches, muscle aches, and other discomforts. PMR addresses these physical symptoms by promoting relaxation.

- Enhanced Concentration: A relaxed body often translates to a clearer mind. Engaging in PMR can help sharpen your focus and concentration by eliminating distracting physical tension.

- Empowerment: PMR is a tool you can use anytime, anywhere. Knowing you have a technique to release tension at your disposal can empower you to navigate stressful situations more effectively.

- Overall Well-Being: Regular practice of PMR contributes to a sense of overall well-being. It's a simple yet effective practice that supports both physical and mental health.

Remember, the key to reaping these benefits is regular practice. Integrating PMR into your routine, especially during times of stress, can make a significant difference in how you feel and cope with life's challenges.

Visualization

Visualization is like creating a mental movie in your mind, and it works through the powerful connection between your thoughts and your body's responses. Here's a breakdown of how visualization works:

- Activation of Brain Regions: When you engage in visualization, specific regions of your brain associated with the senses and emotions become activated. This includes areas responsible for processing visual information and triggering emotional responses.

- Emotional and Physiological Responses: As you vividly imagine a scene or scenario, your brain doesn't just stop at creating images. It also stimulates emotional and physiological responses. For example, if you visualize a calming beach scene, your brain might trigger feelings of relaxation and happiness.

- Activation of the Limbic System: The limbic system, which is involved in emotions and memory, plays a crucial role during visualization. Positive visualizations can activate this system in a way that promotes a sense of well-being and relaxation.

- Neuromuscular Pathways: Visualization doesn't only impact your brain; it extends to your body. As you vividly picture an activity, your brain sends signals to the relevant neuromuscular pathways. This can lead to subtle muscle contractions and movements, mimicking the physical experience of the imagined scenario.

- Stress Reduction: Visualization is known to activate the parasympathetic nervous system, which counteracts the stress response of the sympathetic nervous system. This can result in reduced heart rate, lowered blood pressure, and an overall sense of calm.

- Improved Performance: Athletes often use visualization to enhance their performance. By mentally rehearsing movements and scenarios, they prime their brains and bodies for success. This mental rehearsal can lead to improved physical performance when the actual situation arises.

- Creation of Positive Neural Pathways: Regular visualization can contribute to the creation of positive neural pathways in the brain. The more you visualize positive outcomes, the more your brain becomes accustomed to associating those situations with positive emotions and responses.

- Enhanced Focus and Concentration: Visualization requires concentration and mental focus. Engaging in this practice regularly can train your mind to stay focused on specific goals or scenarios, potentially enhancing your overall concentration skills.

- Reduction of Anxiety: Visualization can be a powerful tool for managing anxiety. By mentally rehearsing and visualizing a calm and controlled response to anxiety-inducing situations, individuals can create a sense of mastery and reduce anticipatory anxiety.

- Facilitation of Goal Achievement: When you visualize yourself achieving your goals, you're essentially programming your mind to work towards them. Visualization can create a sense of motivation and determination, driving you to take the necessary steps to turn your visualized success into reality.

In essence, visualization taps into the intricate connection between the mind and body, leveraging the brain's capacity to influence emotions, physiology, and behavior. Regular and intentional visualization can be a valuable tool for promoting mental well-being and achieving personal and professional goals.

Long-Term Strategies for Maintaining Anxiety Relief

Maintaining a sense of calm and resilience in the face of anxiety is an ongoing journey that requires dedication and the integration of Cognitive Behavioral Therapy (CBT) principles into your daily routine.

Consistent Refresher on CBT Techniques: It's like revisiting the tools in your mental health toolkit. Regularly remind yourself of the CBT techniques you've learned, ensuring they stay sharp and readily available for when you need them.

Progressive Engagement with Fears: Think of it as a gradual climb. Keep exposing yourself to situations that trigger anxiety, but do it at a pace that feels right for you. This consistent exposure helps fortify your resilience over time.

Tweaking Your Lifestyle: Life is dynamic, and so are you. Identify aspects of your lifestyle that contribute to your overall well-being. This might involve making adjustments like prioritizing a good night's sleep, maintaining a balanced diet, and weaving regular exercise into your routine.

Eternal Student of Self-Improvement: Consider yourself a perpetual learner. Stay curious and engaged in the process. Attend maintenance sessions to keep the momentum going, delve into relevant literature to expand your understanding, or explore advanced CBT strategies for continuous personal growth.

In essence, treating anxiety isn't a one-time fix; it's a commitment to an evolving journey. By consistently practicing and integrating CBT into your life, you're not just managing anxiety—you're actively nurturing your mental well-being for the long haul.

As we conclude our exploration of Cognitive Behavioral Therapy (CBT) for anxiety, it's important to recognize that this journey is a dynamic, ongoing process—a dance between understanding, practicing, and evolving. CBT provides not just a set of techniques but a framework for reshaping how we perceive and respond to the challenges of anxiety.

We've ventured through the landscape of anxiety, unraveling its complexities, and discovered how CBT serves as a guiding light. From the roots of anxiety to the transformative power of CBT, we've navigated the intricate pathways of the mind.

Remember, managing anxiety is not about erasing it entirely but about building resilience, fostering self-awareness, and developing a repertoire of practical tools. Whether it's cognitive restructuring, exposure therapy, or mindfulness, these are not just interventions; they're companions in your journey toward lasting well-being.

As you step forward, equipped with the insights and techniques gleaned from CBT, consider this not an endpoint but a new beginning. Embrace the ongoing process of self-discovery and growth, knowing that each step you take contributes to the mosaic of your mental health.

May this chapter be a stepping stone—a reminder that managing anxiety is a continuous, empowering endeavor. The tools you've acquired are not just for moments of distress but for the everyday celebration of resilience and well-being.

Technology and CBT

In our modern world, technology has become a game-changer in the realm of mental health, ushering in a wave of digital tools and applications that seamlessly intertwine with the principles of Cognitive Behavioral Therapy (CBT). In this chapter, we embark on a journey to discover the myriad ways in which technology can become a trusted companion in enhancing and complementing the practices of CBT. Let's explore the innovative avenues where the digital landscape and the human mind converge for a holistic approach to mental well-being.

Digital Tools/Apps for CBT Practice

Let's dive into the world of digital tools and apps that seamlessly align with the principles of Cognitive Behavioral Therapy (CBT), bringing a human touch to the realm of mental well-being:

- ***CBT Apps***: Imagine having a personal guide in your pocket. CBT apps are crafted to make exercises like thought diaries and mood tracking feel like a tailored experience. They offer structured frameworks, turning daily engagement with CBT into a user-friendly and personalized journey.

- ***Virtual Reality (VR) Therapy***: Step into a world where facing fears becomes an immersive experience. VR technology creates controlled environments for exposure therapy, allowing individuals to confront and manage their anxieties in a remarkably realistic yet safe setting.

- ***Meditation and Mindfulness Apps***: Picture infusing your daily routine with moments of tranquillity. Meditation and mindfulness apps bring the essence of CBT to life, offering guided sessions that make cultivating present-moment awareness a seamless and enriching practice.

In this digital era, technology emerges as a supportive companion on the journey to mental well-being. The array of digital tools and applications harmoniously integrates with Cognitive Behavioral Therapy (CBT), offering individuals a personalized and accessible avenue for growth. From thought diaries and mood tracking on CBT apps to the immersive experiences of Virtual Reality Therapy, and the soothing guidance of meditation and mindfulness apps, technology becomes an ally in fostering resilience and self-awareness. As we explore these possibilities, it's evident that the human touch persists, weaving through the fabric of innovation to enhance the therapeutic landscape and make CBT practices more adaptable and relatable to individuals on their unique journeys.

The Role of Teletherapy and Online Resources

In the realm of mental health, the rise of teletherapy, or online therapy, has reshaped the landscape, bringing the transformative power of Cognitive Behavioral Therapy (CBT) to the doorstep of individuals. Through the lens of this chapter, we delve into the myriad advantages teletherapy presents, where the virtual space becomes a haven for exploration and healing.

Firstly, the embrace of video conferencing platforms dismantles the barriers of distance, offering a lifeline for individuals to engage in CBT from the sanctuary of their homes. This democratization of access is a beacon of inclusivity, particularly beneficial for those facing physical constraints or residing in remote areas.

Beyond real-time sessions, the digital realm unfolds a vast array of online CBT courses. These structured programs provide a unique blend of autonomy and guidance, allowing individuals to absorb the principles of CBT at their own pace and weave them seamlessly into the tapestry of their daily lives.

Yet, the magic of the online world doesn't end with structured courses. It extends to the nurturing embrace of supportive online communities. These forums become virtual gathering spaces, where individuals, united by a common quest for mental well-being, share experiences, exchange insights, and find solace in the collective wisdom of peers walking parallel paths on their CBT journey.

In essence, the rise of teletherapy and the digital landscape doesn't diminish the human touch; instead, it amplifies it. It transforms the therapeutic encounter into a more flexible, accessible, and interconnected experience, making the profound benefits of CBT more reachable for everyone, regardless of geographical confines or logistical hurdles. As we navigate the digital realm of teletherapy, we find not just a tool but a compassionate ally, extending the reach of CBT and weaving a tapestry of healing and support in the fabric of our interconnected lives.

Staying Updated with New CBT Developments

Navigating the dynamic landscape of Cognitive Behavioral Therapy (CBT) is akin to embarking on a journey of continuous growth, with ongoing research and development paving the way for transformative advancements. For therapists and individuals eager to stay on the cutting edge of CBT, there exists a vibrant tapestry of possibilities.

Imagine enrolling in professional training programs, where the wisdom of seasoned practitioners converges with the latest insights. These programs become not just educational forums but immersive experiences, where one can absorb the nuances of new CBT techniques and witness their applications in real-world scenarios.

Venturing into the realm of research journals and publications feels like exploring a treasure trove of knowledge.

Regular perusal unveils the latest studies and findings, serving as a compass that guides individuals through the ever-evolving landscape of CBT. It's a journey of discovery, where each piece of information becomes a building block for a deeper understanding and application of CBT principles.

Then, there's the lively arena of conferences and workshops, where professionals gather to share experiences and unveil emerging trends. It's not merely attending events; it's about immersing oneself in an atmosphere pulsating with the collective energy of like-minded individuals. Networking becomes more than an exchange of business cards; it's a chance to forge connections, exchange stories, and gain firsthand knowledge of the evolving practices that shape the future of CBT.

In essence, staying updated with the dynamic field of CBT is not a static obligation; it's an invitation to partake in a living, breathing community of learners and innovators. It's a conscious choice to be woven into the fabric of progress, where each thread of knowledge adds richness to the tapestry of one's professional or personal journey with CBT.

As we conclude our exploration of Chapter 9, we find ourselves at the intersection of tradition and innovation in the realm of Cognitive Behavioral Therapy (CBT). The chapter has been a journey through the evolving landscape of CBT, where age-old principles intertwine seamlessly with cutting-edge technologies and novel approaches.

In embracing the digital era, we've witnessed the transformative potential of technology to enhance CBT practices. From dedicated apps providing structured frameworks for daily engagement with CBT exercises to the immersive experiences offered by Virtual Reality (VR) therapy, technology has become a valuable ally in the pursuit of mental well-being. The integration of meditation and mindfulness apps has not only complemented CBT but has also elevated the mindfulness aspect of therapeutic practices, fostering a more holistic approach to mental health.

Our exploration further led us to the realm of teletherapy, a realm where geographical distances cease to be barriers to mental health support. Through video conferencing platforms, individuals can connect with therapists from the comfort of their homes, making therapy accessible to those with physical limitations or in remote locations. Online CBT courses have democratized the learning experience, allowing individuals to engage with CBT principles at their own pace.

As we delved into the human side of technology, we discovered the importance of supportive online communities. These virtual spaces have become bridges, connecting individuals on their CBT journeys, providing shared experiences, insights, and peer support. The interconnectedness facilitated by these communities reflects the deeply human need for connection and understanding.

In this chapter, the technological advancements and online resources have not replaced the essence of CBT but have rather become powerful tools that amplify its impact. The human touch remains at the core, whether it's the therapist connecting with a client through a screen or individuals finding solace and encouragement in the virtual company of their peers.

As we move forward in our understanding of CBT, let us carry with us the wisdom of tradition and the possibilities of innovation. The journey continues, with each chapter unfolding new dimensions and opportunities for growth in the realm of Cognitive Behavioral Therapy.

Building a Support System

Embarking on the journey of overcoming anxiety takes on a richer and more meaningful hue when we surround ourselves with a strong support system. In this chapter, we delve into the heart of the matter, shining a light on the crucial role that social support plays in navigating the challenges of anxiety. Together, we explore the diverse ways individuals can cultivate a network of understanding and encouragement, creating a tapestry of connections to lean on in times of need.

The Importance of Social Support in Managing Anxiety

Emotional Validation

Having a solid social support system goes beyond just having people around; it's about having a safe space where you can pour out your heart. It's like having this comforting platform where you can be completely honest about how you're

feeling,

whether it's the weight of anxiety or the rollercoaster of emotions that often come with it.

Imagine being able to share your thoughts and fears without fear of judgment, knowing that the people around you genuinely listen and care. When you're understood and your emotions are validated, it's like a soothing balm for the soul. It's this powerful acknowledgment that your experiences are real and valid, which can be incredibly reassuring.

Anxiety often brings with it a sense of isolation, like you're fighting a battle that nobody quite understands. But having a support system changes that narrative. It's like turning on a light in the darkness of isolation, realizing that you're not alone. Feeling understood and validated becomes a beacon of connection, significantly reducing the weight of loneliness that often accompanies anxiety.

Encouragement and Motivation

In the rollercoaster of life, having a supportive network is like having your own cheering squad. When times get tough, this group steps up with words of encouragement, lighting a fire of motivation within you. Their belief in your strength and capacity to overcome anxiety becomes a powerful source of inspiration, fostering a resilience that helps you stand tall against the stormy winds of life's challenges. Their unwavering support acts as a reminder that you're not alone, that together you can conquer the hurdles, and their faith in your ability becomes a beacon guiding you towards greater determination and inner strength.

Perspective and Advice

In times of need, those you trust—whether they're friends, family, or members of your support group—can provide valuable insights and advice that you might not have considered. Their diverse viewpoints bring a richness to your understanding of challenges, paving the way for a more comprehensive approach to finding potential solutions. Having this varied support network enhances your ability to navigate difficulties and discover new paths forward.

Creating a Support Network Including Friends, Family, and Support Groups

Creating a robust support network is a purposeful endeavor that involves nurturing connections with individuals who contribute positively to one's mental well-being.

Family Support

Family members serve as a fundamental pillar of support. Engaging in open conversations about anxiety, coupled with providing education about CBT principles, helps establish an environment that encourages understanding and assistance.

Friendships

Friends play a pivotal role in offering companionship and empathy. The act of sharing personal struggles and triumphs deepens the bond and fosters mutual support in times of need.

Support Groups

Participation in support groups, whether in-person or online, links individuals with others who are navigating similar challenges. These groups serve as shared spaces for empathy, advice, and the exchange of coping strategies, creating a sense of shared understanding and solidarity.

Collaborating with Therapists and Healthcare Providers

Getting professional support is a key element in managing anxiety, and this section delves into the collaborative relationship between individuals and their therapists or healthcare providers.

Therapeutic Alliance

A robust therapeutic alliance between individuals and their therapists is vital for the success of CBT. Open communication and trust create a safe haven for exploring anxiety triggers and implementing therapeutic strategies.

Medication Management

In certain situations, medication might be part of anxiety treatment. Working closely with healthcare providers in medication management ensures a well-rounded approach to anxiety relief.

Regular Check-ins

Maintaining consistent communication with therapists and healthcare providers allows for ongoing assessment and adjustment of treatment plans. Regular check-ins become a platform to address emerging challenges and celebrate the strides made in progress.

As we conclude this journey through the intricate landscape of anxiety management, we find ourselves at the heart of a multifaceted approach—where the intertwining threads of personal resilience, social support, and professional guidance form a tapestry of empowerment.

Recognizing that anxiety is a shared human experience, this chapter illuminated the importance of building a support network and seeking professional assistance. It is within these connections, both personal and professional, that individuals discover the strength to navigate challenges, implement cognitive-behavioral techniques, and forge a path toward lasting well-being. As we bid farewell to this chapter, let us carry forward the understanding that, in the face of anxiety, we are not alone; we are supported, resilient, and equipped with the tools to shape our mental health journey.

Conclusion

Embarking on the journey through Cognitive Behavioral Therapy (CBT) for anxiety relief is like setting sail on a transformative odyssey where the seas of self-discovery, resilience, and personal growth await. As we stand at the conclusion of this enlightening voyage, it's worth pausing to appreciate the profound impact that CBT has on the intricate landscape of our mental well-being.

Picture it as a quest for a calmer mind, a more resilient spirit, and the key to unlocking a profoundly fulfilling life. Through the ebbs and flows of this therapeutic journey, we discover not just tools for managing anxiety but insights that reshape our understanding of ourselves.

In the dance between challenges and triumphs, CBT becomes a guiding light, offering the promise of not just relief but a pathway to lasting transformation and a richer, more meaningful existence.

Summarizing the Journey through CBT and Anxiety Relief

Reflecting on our journey through these chapters, we've embarked on a deep dive into the complex world of anxiety—unveiling its nuances, exploring its various faces, and discovering the transformative potential of Cognitive Behavioral Therapy (CBT). We've traced the contours of the brain's adaptability and dived into advanced techniques, each step shedding light on the profound ways in which CBT can reshape our thoughts and actions, leading to genuine anxiety relief.

In our exploration, we've seamlessly woven CBT into the fabric of daily life, embracing the supportive embrace of technology in mental health, and highlighting the indispensable role of a robust support system. This journey has been nothing short of holistic, intertwining cognitive, behavioral, and emotional threads to create a tapestry of comprehensive anxiety management. As we conclude this expedition, we stand not only equipped with tools for anxiety relief but enriched with a deeper understanding of ourselves and the potential for lasting transformation.

Encouraging Lifelong Learning and Personal Growth

As we wrap up, let's acknowledge that our journey doesn't come to a close; rather, it transforms into an ongoing commitment to lifelong learning and personal growth. CBT isn't just a toolkit of techniques—it's a mindset, a way of navigating challenges with resilience and adaptability

Moving forward, staying curious about the latest in CBT, whether it's fueled by technological advancements or innovative therapeutic strategies, ensures that we continually have the most effective tools at our disposal for navigating the twists and turns of anxiety. Personal growth becomes a perpetual adventure, with each new challenge offering an opportunity to put into practice and refine the skills we've gained through CBT.

Final Thoughts on the Power of CBT and the Potential for a Calmer Mind

As we wrap up our exploration of the power of CBT, it's important to recognize that through embracing these principles, individuals gain the ability to reshape their mental landscape, challenge distorted thoughts, and construct coping mechanisms that stand strong against the storms of anxiety. The promise of a calmer mind isn't just a distant idea—it's a real and achievable outcome, born out of commitment and the practical application of CBT principles.

This journey through CBT is a testament to the resilience of the human spirit and our capacity for positive transformation. It serves as a reminder that, despite the complexities of anxiety, individuals hold the power to change their relationship with their thoughts and emotions.

As you continue on your path toward a calmer mind, let the principles of CBT be your steadfast companions, guiding you through life's ups and downs. With each cognitive technique applied, every step taken in exposure therapy, and the ongoing support from your network, may you not only discover relief from anxiety but also a profound sense of empowerment and a foundation for enduring well-being.

In the realm of CBT and anxiety relief, remember, the journey is not a fixed destination—it's an ongoing, evolving story of personal triumph and the cultivation of a resilient, calm, and empowered mind.

Gratitude Journal

The purpose of a gratitude journal is to foster positive thinking and gratitude. Here's how it works:

- Date: Record the date of the entry.

- Three Good Things: List three positive things that happened.

- Emotions: Note the emotions associated with each positive event.

- Challenge: Identify any challenges or negative aspects of the day.

- Positive Thought: Find a positive or alternative perspective on the challenges.

D a t e :
_____

Three Good Things

___

Emotions

___

Challenge

___

Positive Thought

___

Stress Management Plan

The purpose of this worksheet is to develop a personalized plan for managing stress. Here's how it works:

- Triggers: Identify common stress triggers.

- Coping Strategies: List effective coping strategies for each trigger.

- Support System: Identify individuals or resources for support during stressful times.

- Self-Care Activities: Include regular self-care activities to prevent stress buildup.

- Review: Periodically review and update the plan

as needed.

Triggers

_____

Coping Strategies

_____

Support System

_____

Self-Care Activities

_____

Review

_____

How to Find a Qualified CBT Professional

If you are interested in learning more or exploring CBT, it's important to find a qualified CBT practitioner. Here's how:

Ask for Recommendations

Seek recommendations from friends, family, or colleagues who have had positive experiences with CBT therapists.

Consult Healthcare Providers

Speak to your primary care physician or a mental health professional for referrals. They often have networks of trusted therapists.

Use Online Directories

Explore online directories such as Psychology Today (psychologytoday.com) or the Association for Behavioral and Cognitive Therapies (ABCT) directory.

Check with Insurance Providers

Contact your insurance provider to get a list of therapists covered by your insurance plan. This can help narrow down your options.

Research Online Platforms

Consider online therapy platforms that connect individuals with licensed therapists who offer CBT. Examples include BetterHelp, Talkspace, or online services provided by local mental health organizations.

Local Mental Health Organizations

Reach out to local mental health organizations or community mental health centers. They may provide resources or recommendations.

Verify Credentials

Ensure that the therapist is licensed and has the appropriate credentials. You can check licensing boards and professional associations for verification.

Read Reviews

Look for reviews or testimonials about therapists you are considering. Online platforms and directories often include feedback from clients.

Remember to schedule initial consultations with potential therapists to discuss your needs, ask questions, and determine if they are a good fit for you. It's crucial to feel comfortable and have a good rapport with your therapist for effective therapy.

Recommended Reading

Here is a list of recommended books and research articles on Cognitive Behavioral Therapy (CBT):

Books

"Feeling Good: The New Mood Therapy" by David D. Burns

A classic book that introduces CBT techniques for managing mood and overcoming negative thought patterns.

"The Feeling Good Handbook" by David D. Burns

A companion to "Feeling Good," offering practical exercises and tools for applying CBT in daily life.

"Mind Over Mood: Change How You Feel by Changing the Way You Think" by Dennis Greenberger and Christine A. Padesky

A user-friendly guide that helps individuals learn CBT skills to manage emotions and improve mood.

"Cognitive Behavioural Therapy For Dummies" by Rhena Branch and Rob Willson

An accessible guide that provides an overview of CBT principles and techniques.

"The Anxiety and Worry Workbook: The Cognitive Behavioral Solution" by David A. Clark and Aaron T. Beck

Focuses on CBT strategies for managing anxiety and excessive worry.

Research Articles

"A Meta-Analysis of the Efficacy of Cognitive Therapy for Depression" by Pim Cuijpers et al. (2013)

This meta-analysis examines the effectiveness of cognitive therapy in treating depression.

"The empirical status of cognitive-behavioral therapy: A review of meta-analyses" by Stefan G. Hofmann et al. (2012)

A comprehensive review of meta-analyses on the empirical status of cognitive-behavioral therapy across various disorders.

"Cognitive behavioral therapy in anxiety disorders: Current state of the evidence" by Stefan G. Hofmann et al. (2012)

An overview of the evidence supporting the use of CBT in treating anxiety disorders.

"The Efficacy of Cognitive Behavioral Therapy: A Review of Meta-analyses" by Stefan G. Hofmann et al. (2012)

A review that assesses the efficacy of cognitive-behavioral therapy across different psychiatric disorders.

"The Effectiveness of Cognitive Behavioral Therapy for Generalized Anxiety Disorder: A Meta-Analysis" by Gavin Andrews et al. (2018)

A meta-analysis exploring the effectiveness of CBT in treating generalized anxiety disorder.

These resources cover a range of topics within CBT, from self-help guides to academic reviews. They should provide you with a good starting point for understanding and implementing cognitive-behavioral principles.

www.ingramcontent.com/pod-product-compliance
Lightning Source LLC
LaVergne TN
LVHW021823060526
838201LV00058B/3486